D1565862

DAILY
Encouragement
for Your Marriage

100 Devotions and Prayers

The quoted ideas expressed in this book (but not Scripture verses) are not, in all cases, exact quotations, as some have been edited for clarity and brevity. In all cases, the author has attempted to maintain the speaker's original intent. In some cases, quoted material for this book was obtained from secondary sources, primarily print media. While every effort was made to ensure the accuracy of these sources, the accuracy cannot be guaranteed. For additions, deletions, corrections, or clarifications in future editions of this text, please write Freeman-Smith.

Scripture quotations are taken from:

The Holy Bible, King James Version (KJV)

The Holy Bible, New International Version (NIV) Copyright © 1973, 1978, 1984, by International Bible Society. Used by permission of Zondervan Publishing House. All rights reserved.

The Holy Bible, New King James Version (NKJV) Copyright © 1982 by Thomas Nelson, Inc. Used by permission.

Holy Bible, New Living Translation, (NLT) copyright © 1996. Used by permission of Tyndale House Publishers, Inc., Wheaton, Illinois 60189. All rights reserved.

The Message (MSG)- This edition issued by contractual arrangement with NavPress, a division of The Navigators, U.S.A. Originally published by NavPress in English as THE MESSAGE: The Bible in Contemporary Language copyright 2002-2003 by Eugene Peterson. All rights reserved.

New Century Version®. (NCV) Copyright © 1987, 1988, 1991 by WordPublishing, a division of Thomas Nelson, Inc. All rights reserved. Used by permission.

The New American Standard Bible®, (NASB) Copyright © 1960, 1962, 1963, 1968, 1971, 1972, 1973, 1975, 1977, 1995 by The Lockman Foundation. Used by permission.

The Holman Christian Standard Bible™ (HCSB) Copyright © 1999, 2000, 2001 by Holman Bible Publishers. Used by permission.

Cover Design Kim Russell / Wahoo Designs

Page Layout by Bart Dawson

ISBN 978-1-60587-438-8

Printed in the United States of America

1 2 3 4 5—QGF—16 15 14 13 12

DAILY
Encouragement
for Your Marriage

100 Devotions and Prayers

Introduction

What's the best thing you can do for your marriage? Take a Caribbean cruise? Plan a candlelight dinner? Bring home a box of chocolates? Wrong, wrong, and wrong. The best thing you can do for your marriage is to pray for it early and often.

How do you and your spouse begin the day? Do you awaken early enough to enjoy a few quiet moments together, or are you one of those couples who sleeps until the last possible minute, leaving no time to invest in matters of the heart or the soul? If you and your mate form the habit of getting up early—if both of you start the day by spending a few quiet moments with each other and with God—your marriage will be blessed. After all, the fabric of your marriage is woven together with the threads of habit. And no habit is more important to your family's spiritual health than the habit of daily prayer and devotion to your Creator.

This book contains devotional readings that are intended to help you and your spouse pray for your marriage and set the tone for the rest of your day. The text is divided into 100 chapters. Each chapter contains an essay, Bible verses, quotations, and a prayer, all of which can help you and your beloved focus on the blessings and opportunities that God has placed before you.

During the next 100 days, please try this experiment: Read one chapter each morning with your first cup of coffee, and then discuss the devotional reading with your spouse. This simple act of talking things over—and the act of praying for your marriage—will be helpful to both of you.

Your daily devotional time can be habit-forming, and should be. And, the first few minutes of each day are invaluable. So do yourself and your family a favor: start each day in prayer with God—He deserves no less, and neither, for that matter, do you.

Now these three remain:
faith, hope, and love.
But the greatest of these is love.

1 Corinthians 13:13 HCSB

Chapter 1

The Power of Prayer

So I say to you, keep asking, and it will be given to you.
Keep searching, and you will find.
Keep knocking, and the door will be opened to you.
Luke 11:9 HCSB

I s prayer an integral part of your married life, or is it a hit-or-miss habit? Do you and your spouse "pray without ceasing," or is prayer usually an afterthought? Do you regularly pray together—praying specifically for the health of your marriage—or do you only bow your heads in unison during Sunday morning services? The answer to these questions will determine the quality of your prayer life and, to a surprising extent, the spiritual strength of your marriage.

Andrew Murray observed, "Some people pray just to pray, and some people pray to know God." Your task, along with your spouse, is to pray together, not out of habit or obligation, but out of a sincere desire to know your Heavenly Father.

Through constant prayers, you and your spouse should petition God, you should praise God, and you should seek God's guidance for your marriage and your life.

Prayer changes things, prayer changes people, and prayer changes marriages. So don't limit your prayers to meals or to bedtime. Pray constantly about things great and small. God is listening, and He wants to hear from you—and your spouse—right now.

I have witnessed many attitudes make a positive turnaround through prayer.

John Maxwell

God asks that we worship Him with our concentrated minds as well as with our wills and emotions. A divided and scattered mind is not effective.

Catherine Marshall

Now if any of you lacks wisdom, he should ask God, who gives to all generously and without criticizing, and it will be given to him. But let him ask in faith without doubting. For the doubter is like the surging sea, driven and tossed by the wind.

James 1:5-6 HCSB

— Our Prayer for Today —

We pray to You, Father, because You desire it and because we need it. Prayer not only changes things; it changes us. And it can change our marriage. Help us, Lord, never to face the demands of the day without first spending time with You, and bless our marriage today, tomorrow, and forever. Amen

Chapter 2

Putting God First in Your Marriage

You shall have no other gods before Me.

Exodus 20:3 NKJV

The Bible makes it clear that in marriage, as in every other aspect of life, God should come first. The words of Matthew 6:33 remind us that we should "seek first the kingdom of God and His righteousness." And how can we honor God in this way? By allowing His Son to reign over our hearts and our marriages.

A Christ-centered marriage is an exercise in faith, love, fidelity, trust, understanding, forgiveness, caring, sharing, and encouragement. It requires empathy, tenderness, patience, and perseverance. It is the union of two Christian adults, both of whom are willing to compromise and, when appropriate, to apologize. A Christ-centered marriage requires large quantities of common sense, common courtesy, and uncommon caring. Such a marriage is a joy to behold, a joy to experience, and a blessing forever.

Does Christ truly preside over your marriage, or does He occupy a position of lesser importance? The answer to that question will determine the quality and direction of your lives. When both you and your spouse allow Jesus to reign over your lives, Christ will bless you and your family in wonderful, unexpected ways. So today and every day, make your marriage a model of Christian love, respect, and service. Jesus expects no less, and neither, for that matter, should you.

A man's communication with his wife is dependent upon his communication with the Father.

Stormie Omartian

If God has the power to create and sustain the universe, He is more than able to sustain your marriage and your ministry, your faith and your finances, your hope and your health.

Anne Graham Lotz

So they are no longer two, but one flesh. Therefore what God has joined together, man must not separate.

Matthew 19:6 HCSB

— Our Prayer for Today —

Dear Lord, today, we invite You to reign over our marriage. May Your will be our will. May Your Word be our guide, and may we grow in faith and in wisdom this day and every day. Amen

Chapter 3

The Golden Rule for Couples

Therefore, whatever you want others to do for you,
do also the same for them—
this is the Law and the Prophets.

Matthew 7:12 HCSB

Is the Golden Rule one of the rules that governs your household? Hopefully so. Obeying the Golden Rule is a proven way to improve any relationship, including your marriage. But the reverse is also true: if you or your spouse ignore the Golden Rule altogether, you're headed for trouble, and fast.

Too many marriages become unbalanced when one partner assumes the role of the "taker" while the other partner accepts the role of the "giver." But the healthiest marriages are those in which both parties seek to give more than they get.

Jesus made Himself perfectly clear: He instructed us to treat others in the same way that we want to be treated. That means we must treat other people (including our loved ones) with respect, kindness, and courtesy.

So if you're wondering how you should treat your spouse (or anyone else, for that matter), ask the person you see every time you look into the mirror. The answer you receive will tell you exactly what to do.

The attitude of kindness is everyday stuff like a great pair of sneakers. Not frilly. Not fancy. Just plain and comfortable.

Barbara Johnson

The Golden Rule starts at home, but it should never stop there.

Marie T. Freeman

It is one of the most beautiful compensations of life that no one can sincerely try to help another without helping herself.

Barbara Johnson

And let us not grow weary while doing good, for in due season we shall reap if we do not lose heart.

Galatians 6:9 NKJV

— Our Prayer for Today —

Dear Lord, we thank You for friends and family members who practice the Golden Rule. Because we expect to be treated with kindness, let us be kind. Because we wish to be loved, let us be loving. Because we need forgiveness, let us be merciful. In matters great and small, let us live by the Golden Rule, and let us express our gratitude to those who offer kindness and generosity to us. Amen

Chapter 4

The Firm Foundation

May Your faithful love rest on us, Lord,
for we put our hope in You.
Psalm 33:22 HCSB

God loves you. Period. He loves you more than you can imagine; His affection is deeper and more profound than you can fathom. God made you in His own image and gave you salvation through the person of His Son Jesus Christ. And now, precisely because you are a wondrous creation treasured by God, a crucial question presents itself: What will you do in response to God's love? Will you ignore it or embrace it? Will you return it or neglect it? Will you deny it, or will you share it? These decisions, of course, are yours and yours alone.

When you embrace God's love, you are forever changed. When you embrace God's love, you feel differently about yourself, your loved ones, your marriage, and your world. When you embrace God's love, you share His message—and His mercy—with others.

Have you built every aspect of your life—including your marriage—upon the firm foundation of God's unwavering love for you and yours? If so, you have built your life on the Rock that cannot be moved. And, you have accepted a priceless gift that is yours to share and to keep . . . now and throughout all eternity.

Joy comes from knowing God loves me and knows who I am and where I'm going . . . that my future is secure as I rest in Him.

James Dobson

We can all humbly say in the sincerity of faith, "I am loved; I am called; I am secure."

Franklin Graham

God will never let you be shaken or moved from your place near His heart.

Joni Eareckson Tada

But God demonstrates His own love toward us, in that while we were still sinners, Christ died for us.

Romans 5:8 NKJV

— Our Prayer for Today —

God, You are love. Today and every day, we will return Your love . . . and we will share it with each other and with the world. We will strive to be loving, faithful servants to You and to Your Son, this day and throughout eternity. Amen

Chapter 5

Open Your Heart to Him

If you love Me, you will keep My commandments.

John 14:15 HCSB

C. S. Lewis observed, "A person's spiritual health is exactly proportional to his love for God." If we are to enjoy the spiritual health that God intends for us, we should keep Lewis's words in mind.

Corrie ten Boom noted, "A bird does not know it can fly before it uses its wings. We learn God's love in our hearts as soon as we act upon it." She understood that whenever we worship God with our hearts and our minds, we are blessed by our love for Him and His love for us.

Today, open your heart to the Father. And let your obedience be a fitting response to His never-ending love.

Man was created by God to know and love Him in a permanent, personal relationship.

Anne Graham Lotz

I love Him because He first loved me, and He still does love me, and He will love me forever and ever.

Bill Bright

To love God is to love His will.

Elisabeth Elliot

We love Him because He first loved us.

1 John 4:19 NKJV

— Our Prayer for Today —

Dear Heavenly Father, Your love is infinite and eternal. We praise You, Lord, for Your love, and we will return it this day and throughout eternity. Amen

Chapter 6

Beyond Anxiety

*Be anxious for nothing, but in everything by prayer
and supplication, with thanksgiving,
let your requests be made known to God.*

Philippians 4:6 NKJV

We live in a world that sometimes seems to shift beneath our feet. From time to time, all of us face adversity, discouragement, or disappointment. And, throughout life, we must all endure life-changing personal losses that leave us breathless. When we do, God stands ready to protect us. Psalm 147 promises, "He heals the brokenhearted, and binds their wounds" (v. 3 NIV). When we are troubled, we must call upon God, and, in His own time and according to His own plan, He will heal us.

Are you anxious? Take those anxieties to God. Are you troubled? Take your troubles to Him. Does your world seem to be trembling beneath your feet? Seek protection from the One who cannot be moved. The same God who created the universe will protect you if you ask Him . . . so ask Him.

He treats us as sons, and all He asks in return is that we shall treat Him as a Father whom we can trust without anxiety. We must take the son's place of dependence and trust, and we must let Him keep the father's place of care and responsibility.

Hannah Whitall Smith

Anxiety does not empty tomorrow of its sorrows, but it empties today of its strength.

C. H. Spurgeon

When you are anxious, it means that you aren't trusting God completely; it means that you aren't trusting God to take care of your needs.

Stormie Omartian

Anxiety in the heart of man causes depression, but a good word makes it glad.

Proverbs 12:25 NKJV

— Our Prayer for Today —

Dear Lord, when we are tempted to lose faith in the future, touch our hearts with Your enduring love. And, keep us mindful, Father, that when we place our trust in You, we are secure today and forever. Amen

Chapter 7

Sharing His Love

Show family affection to one another with brotherly love.
Outdo one another in showing honor.
Do not lack diligence; be fervent in spirit;
serve the Lord. Rejoice in hope; be patient in affliction;
be persistent in prayer.

Romans 12:10-12 HCSB

Christ's words leave no room for interpretation: He instructs us to love the Lord with all our hearts and to love our neighbors as we love ourselves. But sometimes, despite our best intentions, we fall short. When we become embittered with ourselves, with our neighbors, or most especially with God, we disobey the One who gave His life for us. And we bring inevitable, needless suffering into our lives.

If we are to please God, we must cleanse ourselves of the negative feelings that separate us from others and from Him. In 1 Corinthians 13, we are told that love is the foundation upon which all our relationships are to be built—love is the foundation of marriage, of family life, of friendship; and it is the foundation of our relationship with the Creator. May we fill our hearts with love; may we never yield to bitterness. And may we praise the Son of God who, in His infinite wisdom, made love His greatest commandment.

You can be sure you are abiding in Christ if you are able to have a Christlike love toward the people that irritate you the most.

Vonette Bright

We've grown to be one soul—two parts; our lives are so intertwined that when some passion stirs your heart, I feel the quake in mine.

Gloria Gaither

May your day be fashioned with joy, sprinkled with dreams, and touched by the miracle of love.

Barbara Johnson

I give you a new commandment: that you love one another. Just as I have loved you, you should also love one another. By this all people will know that you are My disciples, if you have love for one another.

John 13:34-35 HCSB

— Our Prayer for Today —

Lord, You have given us a loving marriage, and we praise You for that gift. We thank You, Father, and we love You. Let the love that we feel for You be reflected through the tenderness that we share with each other and the love that we share with the world. Amen

What's Your Focus?

Let us lay aside every weight and the sin that so easily ensnares us, and run with endurance the race that lies before us, keeping our eyes on Jesus, the source and perfecter of our faith.

Hebrews 12:1-2 HCSB

What is your focus today? Are you both willing to focus your thoughts and energies on God's blessings and upon His will for your lives? Or will you turn your thoughts to other things? Before you answer that question, consider this: God created you in His own image, and He wants you to experience joy and abundance. But, God will not force His joy upon you; you must claim it for yourself.

This day—and every day hereafter—is a chance to celebrate the life, the love, and the marriage that God has given you. It's also a chance to give thanks to the One who has offered you more blessings than you can possibly count.

Today, why not focus your thoughts on the joy that is rightfully yours in Christ? Why not take time to celebrate God's glorious creation? Why not trust your hopes instead of your fears? When you do, you will think optimistically about yourself and your world . . . and you can then share your optimism with others. They'll be better for it, and so will you.

Give me the person who says, "This one thing I do, and not these fifty things I dabble in."

D. L. Moody

Just like commercial organizations need to get their focus off themselves, we as individual Christians and collective churches need to recalibrate our sights on the target God has given us: spiritually lost people.

Bill Hybels

Setting goals is one way you can be sure that you will focus your efforts on the main things so that trivial matters will not become your focus.

Charles Stanley

Therefore don't worry about tomorrow, because tomorrow will worry about itself. Each day has enough trouble of its own.

Matthew 6:34 HCSB

— Our Prayer for Today —

Dear Lord, help us face this day with optimism and hope. And let us focus our thoughts on You, on Your Son, and on Your incomparable gifts. Amen

Chapter 9

The Balancing Act

Then the apostles gathered to Jesus and told Him all things,
both what they had done and what they had taught.
And He said to them, "Come aside by yourselves
to a deserted place and rest a while."
For there were many coming and going,
and they did not even have time to eat.

Mark 6:30-31 NKJV

Face facts: married life is a delicate balancing act, a tightrope walk with over-commitment on one side and under-commitment on the other. And it's up to each of us to walk carefully on that rope, not falling prey to pride (which causes us to attempt too much) or to fear (which causes us to attempt too little).

God's Word promises us the possibility of abundance (John 10:10). And we are far more likely to experience that abundance when we lead balanced lives.

Are you and your mate doing too much—or too little? If so, it's time to have a little chat with God. And if you listen carefully to His instructions, you will strive to achieve a more balanced life, a life that's right for you and your loved ones. When you do, everybody wins.

The balance of affirmation and discipline, freedom and restraint, encouragement and warning is different for each child and season and generation, yet the absolutes of God's Word are necessary and trustworthy no matter how mercuric the time.

Gloria Gaither

You cannot persevere unless there is a trial in your life. There can be no victories without battles; there can be no peaks without valleys. If you want the blessing, you must be prepared to carry the burden and fight the battle. God has to balance privileges with responsibilities, blessings with burdens, or else you and I will become spoiled, pampered children.

Warren Wiersbe

But those who wait on the Lord shall renew their strength; they shall mount up with wings like eagles, they shall run and not be weary, they shall walk and not faint.

Isaiah 40:31 NKJV

— Our Prayer for Today —

Father, let us find contentment and balance. Let Your priorities be our priorities, and when we have done our best, give us the wisdom to place our faith and our trust in You. Amen

Chapter 10

New Beginnings

Then the One seated on the throne said,
"Look! I am making everything new."

Revelation 21:5 HCSB

Each new day offers countless opportunities to serve God, to seek His will, and to obey His teachings. But each day also offers countless opportunities to stray from God's commandments and to wander far from His path.

Sometimes, we wander aimlessly in a wilderness of our own making, but God has better plans for us. And, whenever we ask Him to renew our strength and guide our steps, He does so.

Consider this day a new beginning. Consider it a fresh start, a renewed opportunity to serve your loved ones and your Creator with willing hands and a loving heart. Ask God to renew your sense of purpose as He guides your steps. Today is a glorious opportunity to serve God. Seize that opportunity while you can; tomorrow may indeed be too late.

No matter how badly we have failed, we can always get up and begin again. Our God is the God of new beginnings.

Warren Wiersbe

God is not running an antique shop! He is making all things new!

Vance Havner

Times of travail can be times of birth. Today's suffering can mean tomorrow's glory.

Warren Wiersbe

God, create a clean heart for me and renew a steadfast spirit within me.

Psalm 51:10 HCSB

— Our Prayer for Today —

Dear God, conform us to Your commandments and to Your plans for our lives. Create in each of us a new heart—a heart that embraces the love that You lavish upon us. When we need to change, Lord, change us, and make us new again. Amen

Chapter 11

Called to Account

Therefore, get your minds ready for action,
being self-disciplined, and set your hope completely
on the grace to be brought to you at the revelation of
Jesus Christ. As obedient children, do not be conformed
to the desires of your former ignorance but,
as the One who called you is holy, you also are to be
holy in all your conduct.
1 Peter 1:13-15 HCSB

For most of us, it is a daunting thought: one day, perhaps soon, we'll come face to face with our Heavenly Father, and we'll be called to account for our actions here on earth. Our personal histories will certainly not be surprising to God; He already knows everything about us. But the full scope of our activities may be surprising to us: some of us will be pleasantly surprised; others will not be.

Today, do whatever you can to ensure that your thoughts and your deeds are pleasing to your Creator. Because you will, at some point in the future, be called to account for your actions. And the future may be sooner than you think.

Christians are the citizens of heaven, and while we are on earth, we ought to behave like heaven's citizens.

Warren Wiersbe

Be such a man, and live such a life, that if every man were such as you, and every life a life like yours, this earth would be God's Paradise.

Phillips Brooks

Although God causes all things to work together for good for His children, He still holds us accountable for our behavior.

Kay Arthur

Even a young man is known by his actions—by whether his behavior is pure and upright.

Proverbs 20:11 HCSB

— Our Prayer for Today —

Lord, it is so much easier for us to speak of the righteous life than it is for us to live it. Let us live righteously, and let our actions be consistent with our beliefs, today and always. Amen

Chapter 12

Listening to God

The one who is from God listens to God's words.
This is why you don't listen,
because you are not from God.
John 8:47 HCSB

Sometimes God speaks loudly and clearly. More often, He speaks in a quiet voice—and if you both are wise, you will be listening carefully when He does. To do so, you must carve out quiet moments each day to study His Word and sense His direction.

Can you quiet yourself long enough to listen to your conscience? Are you attuned to the subtle guidance of your intuition? Are you willing to pray sincerely and then to wait quietly for God's response? Hopefully so. Usually God refrains from sending His messages on stone tablets or city billboards. More often, He communicates in more subtle ways. If you both sincerely desire to hear His voice, you must listen carefully, and you must do so in the silent corners of your quiet, willing hearts.

When we come to Jesus stripped of pretensions, with a needy spirit, ready to listen, He meets us at the point of need.

Catherine Marshall

In the soul-searching of our lives, we are to stay quiet so we can hear Him say all that He wants to say to us in our hearts.

Charles Swindoll

We cannot experience the fullness of Christ if we do all the expressing. We must allow God to express His love, will, and truth to us.

Gary Smalley

Be silent before Me.

Isaiah 41:1 HCSB

— Our Prayer for Today —

Lord, help us listen carefully to each other, to our family members, to our friends, and—most importantly—to You. Amen

Chapter 13

Beyond Perfectionism

Be gentle to everyone, able to teach, and patient.

2 Timothy 2:23 HCSB

Marriage is an exercise in patience. From time to time, even the most considerate spouse may do things that worry us or confuse us or anger us. Why? Because even the most considerate spouse is still an imperfect human being, capable of missteps, misdeeds, and mistakes. And it is precisely because our loved ones are human that we learn to be patient with their shortcomings (just as they, too, must be patient with ours).

Are you one of those people who demand perfection from everybody, with the possible exception of yourself? If so, it's time to reassess your expectations. God doesn't expect perfection, and neither should you.

Proverbs 19:11 makes it clear: "People with good sense restrain their anger; they earn esteem by overlooking wrongs" (NLT). So the next time you find yourself drumming your fingers while waiting for your loved one to do the right thing, take a deep breath and ask God for patience. After all, the world unfolds according to God's timetable, not yours. And your loved ones live—and grow—according to their own timetables, too. Sometimes, you must wait patiently, and that's as it should be. After all, think how patient God has been with you.

The happiest people in the world are not those who have no problems, but the people who have learned to live with those things that are less than perfect.

James Dobson

What makes a Christian a Christian is not perfection but forgiveness.

Max Lucado

A patient person [shows] great understanding, but a quick-tempered one promotes foolishness.

Proverbs 14:29 HCSB

— Our Prayer for Today —

Dear Lord, You have taught us that love covers a multitude of shortcomings. Keep us mindful that perfection will be ours in the next world, not in this one. Help us to be accepting of our own imperfections, and give us the wisdom to accept—and even to cherish—the imperfections of those we love. Amen

Chapter 14

Praise Him

Is anyone among you suffering? He should pray.
James 5:13 HCSB

I t's easy to "compartmentalize" our waking hours into a few familiar categories: work, rest, play, family time, and worship. As creatures of habit, we may find ourselves praising God only at particular times of the day or on a particular day of the week. But praise for our Heavenly Father should never be reserved for mealtimes or bedtimes or church. Instead, we should praise God all day, every day, to the greatest extent we can, with thanksgiving in our hearts, and with a song on our lips.

Worship and praise should be woven into the fabric of everything we do; they should not be relegated to a weekly three-hour visit to church on Sunday morning. A. W. Tozer correctly observed, "If you will not worship God seven days a week, you do not worship Him on one day a week."

Do you and your mate praise God many times each day? If so, keep up the good work; if not, it's time to reassess your priorities. When you consider the wonderful things that God has done for you, you'll find the time—or more accurately you'll make the time—to praise Him for all that He has done.

Every time you notice a gift from the Creator, thank Him and praise Him. His works are marvelous, His gifts are beyond understanding, and His love endures forever.

I am to praise God for all things, regardless of where they seem to originate. Doing this is the key to receiving the blessings of God. Praise will wash away my resentments.

Catherine Marshall

Praise Him! Praise Him! Tell of His excellent greatness. Praise Him! Praise Him! Ever in joyful song!

Fanny Crosby

Therefore, through Him let us continually offer up to God a sacrifice of praise, that is, the fruit of our lips that confess His name.

Hebrews 13:15 HCSB

— Our Prayer for Today —

Dear Lord, today and every day we will praise You. We will come to You with hope in our hearts and words of gratitude on our lips. Let our thoughts, our prayers, our words, and our deeds praise You now and forever. Amen

Chapter 15

With All Your Heart

Love one another fervently with a pure heart.
1 Peter 1:22 NKJV

Are you genuinely excited about your marriage? Are you committed to your mate with all your heart? Do you feel good about yourself, your spouse, your kids, and your home life? And do you see each day as a glorious opportunity for your family to serve God and to do His will? Hopefully so. After all, you and your family members were created in God's image, and He has blessed you in more ways than you can count. Now, it's your job to thank Him with words and with deeds.

Psalm 100 reminds us that, as believers, we have every reason to celebrate: "Shout for joy to the LORD, all the earth. Worship the LORD with gladness" (vv. 1-2 NIV). And as you consider the treasures that God has given you—starting with (but not limited to) your marriage and your family—give thanks to your Creator. And when you're finished thanking your Father in heaven, give thanks to your spouse!

The Christian way of life lends stability to marriage because its principles and values naturally produce harmony.

James Dobson

Love cannot be practiced right unless we first exercise it the moment God gives the opportunity.

John Wesley

We've grown to be one soul—two parts; our lives are so intertwined that when some passion stirs your heart, I feel the quake in mine.

Gloria Gaither

And may the Lord make you increase and abound in love to one another and to all.

1 Thessalonians 3:12 NKJV

— Our Prayer for Today —

Dear Lord, Your Word teaches us that our marriage is both sacred and eternal. We thank You, Father, for the love that we share today, tomorrow, and forever. Amen

Courage for Today

Be strong and courageous, and do the work.
Don't be afraid or discouraged, for the Lord God,
my God, is with you.
He won't leave you or forsake you.
1 Chronicles 28:20 HCSB

A storm rose quickly on the Sea of Galilee, and the disciples were afraid. Although they had seen Jesus perform many miracles, the disciples feared for their lives, so they turned to their Savior, and He calmed the waters and the wind.

Sometimes, we, like the disciples, feel threatened by the inevitable storms of life. And when we are fearful, we, too, can turn to Christ for courage and for comfort.

The next time you're afraid, remember that the One who calmed the wind and the waves is also your personal Savior. And remember that the ultimate battle has already been won at Calvary. We, as believers, can live courageously in the promises of our Lord . . . and we should.

If a person fears God, he or she has no reason to fear anything else. On the other hand, if a person does not fear God, then fear becomes a way of life.

Beth Moore

Take courage. We walk in the wilderness today and in the Promised Land tomorrow.

D. L. Moody

When once we are assured that God is good, then there can be nothing left to fear.

Hannah Whitall Smith

Be strong and courageous, all you who put your hope in the Lord.

Psalm 31:24 HCSB

— Our Prayer for Today —

Lord, sometimes this world is a fearful place. Yet, You have promised that You are always with us. Because You are our protector, we are not afraid. Today, Dear Lord, we will live courageously as we place our trust in Your everlasting promises and in Your everlasting love. Amen

Chapter 17

A Foundation of Honesty

These are the things you must do:
Speak truth to one another; render honest and
peaceful judgments in your gates.
Zechariah 8:16 HCSB

Lasting relationships are built upon a foundation of honesty and trust. It has been said on many occasions that honesty is the best policy. For believers, it is far more important to note that honesty is God's policy. And, if we are to be servants worthy of our Savior, Jesus Christ, we must be honest and forthright in all our communications with all people, starting with our spouses.

Sometimes, honesty is difficult; sometimes, honesty is painful; sometimes, honesty makes us feel uncomfortable. Despite these temporary feelings of discomfort, we must make honesty the hallmark of all our relationships; otherwise, we invite needless suffering into our own lives and into the lives of those we love most.

Sometime soon, perhaps even today, you will be tempted to bend the truth or perhaps even to break it. Resist that temptation. Truth is God's way . . . and it must be your way, too.

Much guilt arises in the life of the believer from practicing the chameleon life of environmental adaptation.

Beth Moore

God doesn't expect you to be perfect, but he does insist on complete honesty.

Rick Warren

The single most important element in any human relationship is honesty—with oneself, with God, and with others.

Catherine Marshall

For there is nothing covered, that shall not be revealed; neither hid, that shall not be known. Therefore, whatsoever ye have spoken in darkness shall be heard in the light; and that which ye have spoken in the ear in closets shall be proclaimed upon the housetops.

Luke 12:2-3 KJV

— Our Prayer for Today —

Dear Lord, You command Your children to walk in truth. Give us the courage to speak honestly to each other and to You. And let us walk righteously with Your Son so that others might see Your eternal truths reflected in our words and our deeds. Amen

Chapter 18

A Passion for Life

He did it with all his heart. So he prospered.
2 Chronicles 31:21 NKJV

Are you both passionate about your lives, your loved ones, your work, your marriage, and your Savior? You should be. As thoughtful Christians, you have every reason to live passionately, but sometimes the struggles of everyday living may leave you feeling discouraged or exhausted, or both.

If you fear that your spouse's passion for life is slowly fading away, it's time to slow down, to rest, to recount your blessings, to worship, and to pray. When you feel worried or weary, you must pray fervently for God to renew your sense of wonderment and excitement.

Our world desperately needs faithful believers who are passionate about their lives and their faith. Be such a believer. The world desperately needs your enthusiasm, and just as importantly, you need the experience of sharing it.

When you allow Christ to reign over your heart—when you worship Him with words, thoughts, prayers, and deeds—your life can become a glorious adventure. When you live passionately—and share your passion with others—God will most certainly bless you and yours . . . today and forever.

I don't know about you, but I want to do more than survive life—I want to mount up like the eagle and glide over rocky crags, nest in the tallest of trees, dive for nourishment in the deepest of mountain lakes, and soar on the wings of the wind.

Barbara Johnson

If your heart has grown cold, it is because you have moved away from the fire of His presence.

Beth Moore

When we realize and embrace the Lord's will for us, we will love to do it. We won't want to do anything else. It's a passion.

Franklin Graham

Do not lack diligence; be fervent in spirit; serve the Lord.

Romans 12:11 HCSB

— Our Prayer for Today —

Dear Lord, we thank You for Your countless blessings. We will demonstrate our gratitude by living obediently and passionately. We praise You, Father, for Your blessings, for Your love, and for Your Son. Amen

Chapter 19

The Blame Game

The righteousness of the blameless clears his path,
but the wicked person will fall because of his wickedness.
Proverbs 11:5 HCSB

To blame others for our own problems is the height of futility. Yet the blame game remains (sadly enough) a common marital pastime. Why? Because blaming one's spouse is much easier than fixing oneself. So instead of solving their problems legitimately (by doing the work required to solve them) some married couples are inclined to fret, to blame, and to criticize, while sometimes doing precious little else. When they do, their problems, quite predictably, remain unsolved.

Have either you or your spouse acquired the bad habit of blaming others for problems that you could or should solve yourselves? If so, you are not only disobeying God's Word; you are also wasting your own precious time. So, instead of looking for someone to blame, look for something to fix, and then get busy fixing it. And as you consider your own situations, remember this: God has a way of helping those who help themselves, but He doesn't spend much time helping those who don't.

The main thing is this: we should never blame anyone or anything for our defeats. No matter how evil their intentions may be, they are altogether unable to harm us until we begin to blame them and use them as excuses for our own unbelief.

A. W. Tozer

You'll never win the blame game, so why even bother to play?

Marie T. Freeman

Bitterness is its own prison.

Max Lucado

A man's own foolishness leads him astray, yet his heart rages against the Lord.

Proverbs 19:3 HCSB

— Our Prayer for Today —

Dear Lord, free us from the poison of bitterness and the futility of blame. Let us turn away from destructive emotions so that we may know the perfect peace and spiritual abundance that can be ours through You. Amen

Chapter 20

Counting God's Blessings

For You, Lord, bless the righteous one;
You surround him with favor like a shield.
Psalm 5:12 HCSB

If you both sat down and began counting your blessings, how long would it take? A very, very long time! Your blessings include life, marriage, family, friends, freedom, talents, and possessions, for starters. But, your greatest blessing—a gift that is yours for the asking—is God's gift of salvation through Christ Jesus.

Today, give thanks for your blessings by accepting them fully (with open arms) and by sharing them generously (with thankful hearts).

Billy Graham had this advice: "Think of the blessings we so easily take for granted: Life itself; preservation from danger; every bit of health we enjoy; every hour of liberty; the ability to see, to hear, to speak, to think, and to imagine all this comes from the hand of God." And that's sound advice for Christians—like you—who have been blessed beyond measure.

The Christian life is motivated, not by a list of do's and don'ts, but by the gracious outpouring of God's love and blessing.

Anne Graham Lotz

Grace is an outrageous blessing bestowed freely on a totally undeserving recipient.

Bill Hybels

God is always far more willing to give us good things than we are anxious to have them.

Catherine Marshall

I will make them and the area around My hill a blessing: I will send down showers in their season—showers of blessing.

Ezekiel 34:26 HCSB

— Our Prayer for Today —

Dear Lord, You have given us so much, and we are thankful. We know that every good gift is to be shared with others. We give thanks for Your gifts . . . and we will share them. Amen

Chapter 21

Too Busy?

Don't burn out; keep yourselves fueled and aflame.
Be alert servants of the Master, cheerfully expectant.
Don't quit in hard times; pray all the harder.

Romans 12:11-12 MSG

Are you both making time each day to praise God and to study His Word? If so, you know firsthand the blessings that He offers those who worship Him consistently and sincerely. But, if you have unintentionally allowed the hustle and bustle of your busy day to come between you and your Creator, then you must slow down, take a deep breath, and rearrange your priorities.

God loved this world so much that He sent His Son to save it. And now only one real question remains for you: what will you do in response to God's love? The answer should be obvious: God must come first in your life. He is the giver of all good things, and He is the One who sent His Son so that you might have eternal life. He deserves your prayers, your obedience, your stewardship, and your love—and He deserves these things all day every day, not just on Sunday mornings.

The busier we are, the easier it is to worry, the greater the temptation to worry, the greater the need to be alone with God.

Charles Stanley

Noise and words and frenzied, hectic schedules dull our senses, closing our ears to His still, small voice and making us numb to His touch.

Charles Swindoll

Frustration is not the will of God. There is time to do anything and everything that God wants us to do.

Elisabeth Elliot

The plans of the diligent certainly lead to profit, but anyone who is reckless only becomes poor.

Proverbs 21:5 HCSB

— Our Prayer for Today —

Dear Lord, when the quickening pace of life leaves us with little time for worship or for praise, help us reorder our priorities. When the demands of the day leave us distracted and discouraged, let us turn to Jesus for the peace that only He can give. And then, when we have accepted the spiritual abundance that can be ours through Christ, let us share His message and His love. Amen

Chapter 22

Enthusiasm Now

*Whatever you do, do it enthusiastically,
as something done for the Lord and not for men.*

Colossians 3:23 HCSB

Do you and your spouse see each day as a glorious opportunity to serve God and to do His will? Are you genuinely enthused about life, or do you struggle through each day giving scarcely a thought to God's blessings? Are you constantly praising God for His gifts, and are you sharing His Good News with the world? Are you excited about your marriage and about the possibilities for service that God has placed before you, whether at home, at work, or at church? You should be.

You and your spouse are the recipients of Christ's sacrificial love. Accept it enthusiastically and share it fervently. Jesus deserves your enthusiasm; the world deserves it; and you deserve the experience of sharing it with the world.

It is a remarkable thing that some of the most optimistic and enthusiastic people you will meet are those who have been through intense suffering.

Warren Wiersbe

Wherever you are, be all there. Live to the hilt every situation you believe to be the will of God.

Jim Elliot

When we wholeheartedly commit ourselves to God, there is nothing mediocre or run-of-the-mill about us. To live for Christ is to be passionate about our Lord and about our lives.

Jim Gallery

Do not lack diligence; be fervent in spirit; serve the Lord.

Romans 12:11 HCSB

— Our Prayer for Today —

Dear Lord, You have promised that we can experience abundance and joy. Today and every day, we will strive to maintain our passion for life, our passion for each other, and our passion for You. We will be enthusiastic followers of Your Son, and we will share His Good News—and His love—with all those who cross our paths. Amen

Chapter 23

Problem-Solving 101

Let not your heart be troubled:
ye believe in God, believe also in me.

John 14:1 KJV

From time to time, all of us face problems, disappointments, heartaches, and loss. Old Man Trouble pays periodic visits to each of us; none of us are exempt, and neither are our marriages. When we are troubled, God stands ready and willing to protect us. Our responsibility, of course, is to ask for His healing touch. When we call upon Him in heartfelt prayer, He will answer—in His own time and in accordance with His own perfect plan.

When we encounter problems or misunderstandings in our relationships, we must work to heal those problems sooner rather than later. Marital problems, like all problems, are most easily solved when they are new and small. That's why wise couples do the hard work of addressing their problems honestly, forthrightly, and quickly (even when they might prefer to downplay their difficulties or ignore those difficulties altogether).

Ignoring problems instead of fixing them is tempting but irresponsible. After all, if we won't solve our problems, who will? Or should?

In summary, the hallmark of a healthy marriage is not the absence of problems but a willingness to solve those problems now. May you live—and love—accordingly.

Often, in the midst of great problems, we stop short of the real blessing God has for us, which is a fresh vision of who He is.

Anne Graham Lotz

Dear friends, when the fiery ordeal arises among you to test you, don't be surprised by it, as if something unusual were happening to you. Instead, as you share in the sufferings of the Messiah rejoice, so that you may also rejoice with great joy at the revelation of His glory.

1 Peter 4:12-13 HCSB

— Our Prayer for Today —

Dear Lord, sometimes our problems are simply too big for us, but they are never too big for You. We will turn our troubles over to You, Father, and we will trust You to guide us and to protect us today, tomorrow, and for all eternity. Amen

Chapter 24

Obey Him

You shall walk after the Lord your God and fear Him,
and keep His commandments and obey His voice,
and you shall serve Him and hold fast to Him.
Deuteronomy 13:4 NKJV

Obedience to God is determined not by words but by deeds. Talking about righteousness is easy; living righteously is far more difficult, especially in today's temptation-filled world.

Since God created Adam and Eve, we human beings have been rebelling against our Creator. Why? Because we are unwilling to trust God's Word, and we are unwilling to follow His commandments. God has given us a guidebook for righteous living called the Holy Bible. It contains thorough instructions that, if followed, lead to fulfillment, righteousness, and salvation. But, if we choose to ignore God's commandments, the results are as predictable as they are tragic.

Unless we are willing to abide by God's laws, all of our righteous proclamations ring hollow. How can we best proclaim our love for the Lord? By obeying Him. And, for further instructions, read the manual.

A life of obedience is not a life of following a list of do's and don'ts, but it is allowing God to be original in our lives.

Vonette Bright

God's mark is on everything that obeys Him.

Martin Luther

The surest evidence of our love to Christ is obedience to the laws of Christ. Love is the root; obedience is the fruit.

Matthew Henry

And the world with its lust is passing away, but the one who does God's will remains forever.

1 John 2:17 HCSB

— Our Prayer for Today —

Heavenly Father, when we turn our thoughts away from You and Your Word, we suffer. But when we obey Your commandments—when we place our trust in You—we are secure. Let us live according to Your commandments. Direct us far from the temptations and distractions of this world. And, let us discover Your will and follow it, Dear Lord, this day and always. Amen

Chapter 25

Best Friends

As iron sharpens iron, so people can improve each other.
Proverbs 27:17 NCV

D o you want your love to last forever? If so, here's a time-tested prescription for a blissfully happy marriage: make certain that your spouse is your best friend.

Genuine friendship between a husband and wife should be treasured and nurtured. As Christians, we are commanded to love one another. The familiar words of 1 Corinthians 13:2 remind us that love and charity are among God's greatest gifts: "And though I have the gift of prophecy, and understand all mysteries, and all knowledge; and though I have all faith, so that I could remove mountains, and have not charity, I am nothing" (KJV).

Is your spouse your best friend? If so, you are immensely blessed by God—never take this gift for granted. So today, remember the important role that friendship plays in your marriage. That friendship is, after all, a glorious gift, praised by God. Give thanks for that gift and nurture it.

There is no more lovely, friendly, and charming relationship, communion, or company than a good marriage.

Martin Luther

The bond of human friendship has a sweetness of its own, binding many souls together as one.

St. Augustine

In friendship, God opens your eyes to the glories of Himself.

Joni Eareckson Tada

Beloved, if God so loved us, we also ought to love one another.

1 John 4:11 NKJV

— Our Prayer for Today —

Dear Lord, today and every day, let our marriage be a celebration of love, respect, consideration, obedience, and friendship. Amen

Chapter 26

Beyond Anger

A gentle answer turns away anger,
but a harsh word stirs up wrath.

Proverbs 15:1 HCSB

The frustrations of everyday living can sometimes get the better of us, and we allow minor disappointments to cause us major problems. When we allow ourselves to become overly irritated by the inevitable ups and downs of life, we become overstressed, overheated, overanxious, and just plain angry.

If you allow yourself to become angry, you are certain to defeat at least one person: yourself. And if you allow the minor frustrations of everyday life to hijack your emotions, you do harm to yourself and to your loved ones. So today and every day, guard yourself against the kind of angry thinking that inevitably takes a toll on your emotions and your marriage.

As the old saying goes, "Anger usually improves nothing but the arch of a cat's back." So don't allow feelings of anger or frustration to rule your life, or, for that matter, your home—your life is too short and your family too precious for that. Instead of losing your temper, obey God's Word by turning away from anger today and every day. You'll be glad you did, and so will your family and friends.

Get rid of the poison of built-up anger and the acid of long-term resentment.

Charles Swindoll

Anger unresolved will only bring you woe.

Kay Arthur

What is hatred, after all, other than anger that was allowed to remain, that has become ingrained and deep-rooted? What was anger when it was fresh becomes hatred when it is aged.

St. Augustine

So then, my beloved brethren, let every man be swift to hear, slow to speak, slow to wrath; for the wrath of man does not produce the righteousness of God.

James 1:19-20 NKJV

— Our Prayer for Today —

Lord, sometimes, in moments of frustration, we become angry. When we fall prey to irrational anger, give us inner calm. Let us show our thankfulness to You by offering forgiveness to each other. And, when we do, let others see Your love reflected through our words and our deeds. Amen

Chapter 27

Giving More

A new commandment I give to you,
that you love one another; as I have loved you,
that you also love one another.

John 13:34 NKJV

When it comes to your marriage, who's Number One: you or your spouse? If you consistently place your own needs above the needs of your loved one, you're probably headed for trouble, and fast.

Jesus taught that the most esteemed men and women are not those who say "me first." Christ instructed us that the greatest among us will be "servants of all" (Mark 9:35). And these words are especially true in the context of marriage.

Are you willing to contribute unselfishly to the well-being of your loved one? And are you willing to do so without constantly comparing your own good deeds to the deeds of your spouse? If so, your marriage will be blessed by your unselfishness. If not, it's time to heed this word of advice: The best way to make love last is by saying "you first"—and meaning it.

It's not difficult to make an impact on your world. All you really have to do is put the needs of others ahead of your own. You can make a difference with a little time and a big heart.

James Dobson

When you invite God to become your partner, you invite untold blessings into your life.

Marie T. Freeman

Honor all people. Love the brotherhood. Fear God. Honor the king.

1 Peter 2:17 NKJV

— Our Prayer for Today —

Dear Lord, let us treat each other as we wish to be treated. Because we expect to receive kindness, let us be kind. Because we wish to be loved, let us be loving. Because we need forgiveness, let us be merciful. In all things, Lord, let us live by the Golden Rule, and let us teach that rule to others through our words and our deeds. Amen

Chapter 28

Embracing Your Future

Do not boast about tomorrow,
for you do not know what a day may bring forth.
Proverbs 27:1 NKJV

Sometimes the future seems bright, and sometimes it does not. Yet even when we cannot see the possibilities of tomorrow, God can. Our challenge is to trust ourselves to do the best work we can, and then to trust God to do the rest.

When we trust God, we should trust Him without reservation. We should steel ourselves against the inevitable disappointments of the day, secure in the knowledge that our Heavenly Father has a plan for the future that is brighter than we can imagine.

Are you willing to look to the future with trust and confidence? Hopefully so, because the future should not be feared; it should be embraced. And it most certainly should be embraced by you.

Don't ever forget there are more firsts to come.

Dennis Swanberg

The Christian believes in a fabulous future.

Billy Graham

Never be afraid to trust an unknown future to a known God.

Corrie ten Boom

"For I know the plans I have for you"—[this is] the Lord's declaration—"plans for [your] welfare, not for disaster, to give you a future and a hope."

Jeremiah 29:11 HCSB

— Our Prayer for Today —

Lord, sometimes life is so difficult that the future seems foreboding. And sometimes we may lose hope. But with You, there is always hope. Today, we will keep Your promises in our hearts, and we will trust the future to You. Amen

Chapter 29

Genuine Peace

*Peace I leave with you. My peace I give to you.
I do not give to you as the world gives.
Your heart must not be troubled or fearful.*

John 14:27 HCSB

Peace with God. Peace with self. Peace with others. Do you possess that kind of peace? Have you found the genuine peace that can be yours through Jesus Christ—and have you allowed Him to rule over your marriage—or are you still rushing after the illusion of "peace and happiness" that the world promises but cannot deliver? The words of John 14:27 remind us that Jesus offers us peace, not as the world gives, but as He alone gives. Our challenge is to accept Christ's peace into our hearts and then, as best we can, to share His peace with our neighbors.

Today, as a gift to yourself and your loved ones, claim the inner peace that is your spiritual birthright: the peace of Jesus Christ. It is offered freely; it has been paid for in full; it is yours for the asking. So ask. And then share.

God is in control of history; it's His story. Doesn't that give you a great peace—especially when world events seem so tumultuous and insane?

Kay Arthur

Look around you and you'll be distressed; look within yourself and you'll be depressed; look at Jesus, and you'll be at rest!

Corrie ten Boom

"My peace I give unto you"; it is a peace all over from the crown of the head to the sole of the feet, an irrepressible confidence.

Oswald Chambers

For the mind-set of the flesh is death, but the mind-set of the Spirit is life and peace.

Romans 8:6 HCSB

— Our Prayer for Today —

Dear Lord, let us accept the peace and abundance that You offer through Your Son Jesus. You are the Giver of all things good, Father, and You give us peace when we draw close to You. Help us to trust Your will, to follow Your commands, and to accept Your peace, today and forever. Amen

Chapter 30

Beyond Materialism

Do not love the world or the things in the world.
If anyone loves the world,
the love of the Father is not in him.

1 John 2:15 NKJV

arthly riches are temporary. Spiritual riches, on the other hand, are everlasting. Yet all too often, we focus our thoughts and energies on the accumulation of earthly treasures, leaving precious little time for anything else.

Far too many marriages are weighted down by endless concerns about money and possessions. Too many couples mistakenly focus their thoughts and efforts on newer cars, better clothes, and bigger houses. The results of these misplaced priorities are always unfortunate, and sometimes tragic.

Certainly we all need the basic necessities of life, but once we meet those needs for our families and ourselves, the piling up of possessions creates more problems than it solves. Our real riches are not of this world: we are never really rich until we are rich in spirit.

Do you find yourself wrapped up in the concerns of the material world? If so, it's time for you and your spouse to sit down and have a heart-to-heart talk about "stuff." When you do, you should reorder your priorities by turning away from materialism and back to God.

Then, you can begin storing up riches that will endure throughout eternity: the spiritual kind.

As faithful stewards of what we have, ought we not to give earnest thought to our staggering surplus?

Elisabeth Elliot

The cross is laid on every Christian. It begins with the call to abandon the attachments of this world.

Dietrich Bonhoeffer

Greed is evil because it substitutes material things for the place of honor that the Creator ought to have in an individual's life.

Charles Stanley

He who trusts in his riches will fall, but the righteous will flourish.

Proverbs 11:28 NKJV

— Our Prayer for Today —

Heavenly Father, when we focus intently upon You, we are blessed. When we focus too intently on the acquisition of material possessions, we are troubled. Make our priorities pleasing to You, Father, and make us worthy servants of Your Son. Amen

Chapter 31

Beyond Bitterness

*But I tell you, everyone who is angry with his brother
will be subject to judgment.*
Matthew 5:22 HCSB

Bitterness is a spiritual sickness. It will consume your soul; it is dangerous to your marriage and to your emotional health. It can destroy you if you let it . . . so don't let it!

If you are caught up in intense feelings of anger or resentment, you know all too well the destructive power of these emotions. How can you rid yourself of these feelings? First, you must prayerfully ask God to cleanse your heart. Then, you must learn to catch yourself whenever thoughts of bitterness or hatred begin to attack you. Your challenge is this: You must learn to resist negative thoughts before they hijack your emotions.

Matthew 5:22 teaches us that if we judge our brothers and sisters, we, too, will be subject to judgment. Let us refrain, then, from judging our neighbors. Instead, let us forgive them and love them, while leaving their judgment to a far more capable authority: the One who sits on His throne in heaven.

Bitterness is the greatest barrier to friendship with God.

Rick Warren

Bitterness is the trap that snares the hunter.

Max Lucado

By not forgiving, by not letting wrongs go, we aren't getting back at anyone. We are merely punishing ourselves by barricading our own hearts.

Jim Cymbala

All bitterness, anger and wrath, insult and slander must be removed from you, along with all wickedness. And be kind and compassionate to one another, forgiving one another, just as God also forgave you in Christ.

Ephesians 4:31-32 HCSB

— Our Prayer for Today —

Heavenly Father, free us from anger and bitterness. When we are angry, we cannot feel Your peace. When we are bitter, we cannot sense Your presence. Let us turn away from bitterness and regret as we claim the spiritual abundance that You offer through the gift of Your Son. Amen

A Willingness to Listen

My dearly loved brothers, understand this:
everyone must be quick to hear,
slow to speak, and slow to anger.

James 1:19 HCSB

What a blessing it is when our loved ones genuinely seek to understand who we are and what we think. Just as we wish to be understood by others, so, too, should we seek to understand the hopes and dreams of our spouses and our family members.

Are you in the habit of listening to your mate? Do you listen carefully (not superficially), and do you take time to think about the things that you hear? If so, you're building a stronger marriage. But if you allow the obligations of everyday living to interfere with the communications you share with your spouse, it's time to reorder your priorities.

You live in a busy world, a place where it is all too easy to overlook the needs of others, but God's Word instructs you to do otherwise. In the Gospel of Matthew, Jesus declares, "In everything, therefore, treat people the same way you want them to treat you, for this is the Law and the Prophets" (Matthew 7:12 NASB). This is the Golden Rule, and it should govern your marriage.

Do you want your voice to be heard? Of course you do. So, in adherence with the Golden Rule, you should also let your spouse's voice be heard—by you.

The first service one owes to others in the fellowship consists in listening to them. Just as love of God begins in listening to His Word, so the beginning of love for the brethren is learning to listen to them.

Dietrich Bonhoeffer

One of the best ways to encourage someone who's hurting is with your ears—by listening.

Barbara Johnson

A fool's way is right in his own eyes, but whoever listens to counsel is wise.

Proverbs 12:15 HCSB

— Our Prayer for Today —

Dear Lord, let us listen carefully to each other and to You. When we listen, we learn. So, today and every day, let us strive to understand each other as we follow in the footsteps of Your Son. Amen

Chapter 33

A High Priority?

You will be a good servant of Christ Jesus,
nourished by the words of the faith and of the good
teaching that you have followed.

1 Timothy 4:6 HCSB

Is Bible study a high priority for you and your family?
The answer to this simple question will determine,
to a surprising extent, the quality of your lives and
the direction of your faith.

As a family, you must decide whether God's Word
will be a bright spotlight that guides your path every
day or a tiny nightlight that occasionally flickers in the
dark. The decision to study the Bible—or not—is yours
individually and collectively. But make no mistake:
how your family chooses to use the Bible will have a
profound impact on every member of the household.

George Mueller observed, "The vigor of our
spiritual lives will be in exact proportion to the place
held by the Bible in our lives and in our thoughts."
Think of it like this: the more you use your Bible, the
more God uses you.

Perhaps your bookshelf is filled with Bibles that
are read infrequently. If so, remember the old saying,
"A Bible in the hand is worth two in the bookcase."
Or perhaps yours is one of those families that is simply

"too busy" to find time for a daily dose of prayer and Bible study. If so, remember the old adage, "It's hard to stumble when you're on your knees."

God's Word can be a roadmap to a place of righteousness and abundance. Make it your family's roadmap. God's wisdom can be a light to guide your steps. Claim it as your family's light today, tomorrow, and every day of your life—and then walk confidently in the footsteps of God's only begotten Son.

Since the Christian's Point of Reference is the Bible, it's a happy couple who look there for guidance.

Ruth Bell Graham

But grow in the grace and knowledge of our Lord and Savior Jesus Christ. To Him be the glory both now and forever. Amen.

2 Peter 3:18 NKJV

— Our Prayer for Today —

Heavenly Father, Your Holy Word is a light unto the world; we will study it, trust it, and share it. In all that we do, help us be worthy witnesses for You as we share the Good News of Your perfect Son and Your perfect Word. Amen

Chapter 34

Comforting Others

*Blessed be the God and Father of our Lord Jesus Christ,
the Father of mercies and the God of all comfort. He
comforts us in all our affliction, so that we may be able to
comfort those who are in any kind of affliction, through the
comfort we ourselves receive from God.*

2 Corinthians 1:3-4 HCSB

We live in a world that is, on occasion, a frightening place. Sometimes, we sustain life-changing losses that are so profound and so tragic that it seems we could never recover. But, with God's help and with the help of encouraging family members and friends, we can recover.

In times of need, friends comfort friends. Our task, as Christians, is to comfort our families and friends by sharing not only our own courage but also the peace and assurance of our Lord and Savior, Christ Jesus. As the renowned revivalist Vance Havner observed, "No journey is complete that does not lead through some dark valleys. We can properly comfort others only with the comfort wherewith we ourselves have been comforted of God."

In times of adversity, we are wise to remember the words of Jesus, who, when He walked on the waters, reassured His disciples, saying, "Take courage! It is I.

Don't be afraid" (Matthew 14:27 NIV). Then, with Christ on His throne and trusted friends at our side, we can face our fears with courage and faith.

Discouraged people don't need critics. They hurt enough already. They don't need more guilt or piled-on distress. They need encouragement. They need a refuge, a willing, caring, available someone.

Charles Swindoll

God's promises are medicine for the broken heart. Let Him comfort you. And, after He has comforted you, try to share that comfort with somebody else. It will do both of you good.

Warren Wiersbe

Carry one another's burdens; in this way you will fulfill the law of Christ.

Galatians 6:2 HCSB

— Our Prayer for Today —

Heavenly Father, sometimes this world can be a difficult place indeed. Let us be beacons of encouragement to those who have lost hope. Let us comfort those who grieve. And let us share Your love and spread Your Word to a world that needs both. Amen

Chapter 35

Seeking God's Approval

For the eyes of the Lord are over the righteous,
and his ears are open unto their prayers:
but the face of the Lord is against them that do evil.

1 Peter 3:12 KJV

As Christians, we are called to walk with God and obey His commandments. When we seek righteousness in our own lives—and when we enjoy the companionship of those who do likewise—we reap the spiritual rewards that God has promised us. When we behave ourselves as godly men and women, when we live righteously and according to God's commandments, He blesses us in ways that we cannot fully understand.

Would you like a time-tested formula for a successful marriage and a successful life? Here is a formula that is proven and true: Seek God's approval in every aspect of your life. Does this sound too simple? Perhaps it is simple, but it is also the only way to reap the marvelous riches that God has in store for you.

So today, take every step of your journey with God as your traveling companion. Read His Word and follow His commandments. Support only those activities that further God's kingdom and your spiritual growth. Be an example of righteousness to your spouse, to your neighbors, and to your children. Then, reap the blessings that God has promised to all those who live according to His will and His Word.

We must appropriate the tender mercy of God every day after conversion, or problems quickly develop. We need his grace daily in order to live a righteous life.

Jim Cymbala

As you walk by faith, you live a righteous life, for righteousness is always by faith.

Kay Arthur

A man who lives right, and is right, has more power in his silence than another has by his words.

Phillips Brooks

Blessed are the pure in heart, for they shall see God.

Matthew 5:8 NKJV

— Our Prayer for Today —

Dear Lord, this world is filled with so many temptations, distractions, and frustrations. When we turn our thoughts away from You and Your Word, we suffer. But when we turn our thoughts and prayers toward You and Your Son, we are secure. Direct us, Father, today and every day that we live. Amen

Chapter 36

Sharing Your Testimony

But the following night the Lord stood by him and said,
"Be of good cheer, Paul; for as you have testified for Me."
Acts 23:11 NKJV

Have you and your spouse made the decision to allow Christ to reign over your hearts? If so, you both have important stories to tell.

In his second letter to Timothy, Paul shares a message to believers of every generation when he writes, "God has not given us a spirit of fear and timidity" (1:7 NLT). Paul's meaning is clear: When sharing our testimonies, we, as Christians, must be courageous, forthright, and unashamed. But sometimes, because we are fearful that we might be rebuffed, we may be slow to acknowledge the changes that Christ has made in our lives. Nonetheless, we must rise above our fears in order to share the story of Jesus with a world that desperately needs to hear His story.

When we let other people know the details of our faith, we assume an important responsibility: the responsibility of making certain that our actions give credence to our words. Once we have shared our testimonies, we must also be willing to serve as shining examples of righteousness—undeniable examples of the changes that Jesus makes in the lives of those who accept Him as their Savior.

Are you willing to follow in the footsteps of Jesus? If so, you must also be willing to talk about Him. And make no mistake: the time to express your belief in Him is now. You know how He has touched your own heart; help Him do the same for others.

To stand in an uncaring world and say, "See, here is the Christ" is a daring act of courage.

Calvin Miller

The sermon of your life in tough times ministers to people more powerfully than the most eloquent speaker.

Bill Bright

Set apart the Messiah as Lord in your hearts, and always be ready to give a defense to anyone who asks you a reason for the hope that is in you.

1 Peter 3:15 HCSB

— Our Prayer for Today —

Dear Lord, let us share the Good News of Your Son Jesus; let the lives that we live and the words that we speak bear testimony to our faith in Him. Help us share our faith with others so that they, too, might dedicate their lives to Christ and receive His eternal gifts. Amen

Chapter 37

Thank Him

*In everything give thanks; for this is the will
of God in Christ Jesus for you.*

1 Thessalonians 5:18 NKJV

Your life and your marriage are gifts from God: celebrate them and give thanks. When you celebrate the gifts of life and love, your thankful heart will serve as a powerful blessing to your loved ones.

Every good gift comes from God. As believers who have been saved by a risen Christ, we owe unending thanksgiving to our Heavenly Father. Yet sometimes, amid the crush of everyday living, we simply don't stop long enough to pause and thank our Creator for His countless blessings. As Christians, we are blessed beyond measure. Thus, thanksgiving should become a habit, a regular part of our daily routines.

Christian believers can face the inevitable challenges of married life armed with the joy of Christ and the promise of salvation. So whatever this day holds for you, begin it and end it with God as your partner and Christ as your Savior. And throughout the day, give thanks to the One who created you and saved you. Place God squarely at the center of your marriage and your life. Then celebrate! God's love for you is infinite. Accept it joyously and be thankful.

God has promised that if we harvest well with the tools of thanksgiving, there will be seeds for planting in the spring.

Gloria Gaither

Thank God every morning when you get up that you have something to do that day which must be done, whether you like it or not.

Charles Kingsley

Thanksgiving is good but Thanksliving is better.

Jim Gallery

We always thank God, the Father of our Lord Jesus Christ, when we pray for you.

Colossians 1:3 HCSB

— Our Prayer for Today —

Heavenly Father, Your gifts are greater than we can imagine. Let us live each day with thanksgiving in our hearts and praise on our lips. Thank You for the gift of Your Son and for the promise of eternal life. Today and every day, let us share the joyous news of Jesus Christ, and let our lives be testimonies to His love and His grace. Amen

Chapter 38

Trust the Shepherd

*My cup runs over. Surely goodness
and mercy shall follow me all the days of my life;
and I will dwell in the house of the Lord forever.*

Psalm 23:5-6 NKJV

O pen your Bible to its center, and you'll find the Book of Psalms. In it are some of the most beautiful words ever translated into the English language, with none more beautiful than the 23rd Psalm. David describes God as being like a shepherd who cares for His flock. No wonder these verses have provided comfort and hope for generations of believers.

You are precious in the eyes of God. You are His priceless creation, made in His image and protected by Him. God watches over every step you make and every breath you take, so you need never be afraid. But sometimes, fear has a way of slipping into the minds and hearts of even the most devout believers. You are no exception.

On occasion, you will confront circumstances that trouble you to the very core of your soul. When you are afraid, trust in God. When you are worried, turn your concerns over to Him. When you are anxious, be still and listen for the quiet assurance of God's promises. And then, place your life in His hands. He is your Shepherd today and throughout eternity. Trust the Shepherd.

Since the Lord is your shepherd, what are you worried about?

Marie T. Freeman

You can better understand the 23rd Psalm when you are acquainted with the Shepherd.

Anonymous

The Lord is my shepherd; I shall not want. He makes me to lie down in green pastures; He leads me beside the still waters. He restores my soul.

Psalm 23:1-3 NKJV

— Our Prayer for Today —

Lord, You are our Shepherd. You care for us; You love us; You protect us. With You as our shield, we have no reason to be afraid. But sometimes, Lord, we are fearful. In times of uncertainty, we feel threatened. In times of sorrow, we weep. In times of trouble, we become angry. Help us, Lord, to lean not upon ourselves, but upon You. Keep us ever mindful of Your promises, and let us trust You always. You are our Shepherd, Lord; and we are Yours forever. Amen

Chapter 39

Acceptance Now

Should I not drink the cup that the Father has given Me?
John 18:11 HCSB

The American theologian Reinhold Niebuhr composed a profoundly simple verse that came to be known as the Serenity Prayer: "God, grant me the serenity to accept the things I cannot change, the courage to change the things I can, and the wisdom to know the difference." Niebuhr's words are far easier to recite than they are to live by. Why? Because most of us want life to unfold in accordance with our own wishes and timetables. But sometimes God has other plans.

Author Hannah Whitall Smith observed, "How changed our lives would be if we could only fly through the days on wings of surrender and trust!" These words remind us that even when we cannot understand the workings of God, we must trust Him and accept His will.

So if you and your spouse have encountered unfortunate circumstances that are beyond your power to control, accept those circumstances . . . and trust God. When you do, you can be comforted in the knowledge that your Creator is both loving and wise, and that He understands His plans perfectly, even when you do not.

I am truly grateful that faith enables me to move past the question of "Why?"

Zig Ziglar

The key to contentment is to consider. Consider who you are and be satisfied with that. Consider what you have and be satisfied with that. Consider what God's doing and be satisfied with that.

Luci Swindoll

The more comfortable we are with mystery in our journey, the more rest we will know along the way.

John Eldredge

He is the Lord. He will do what He thinks is good.

1 Samuel 3:18 HCSB

— Our Prayer for Today —

Dear Lord, when we are discouraged, give us hope. When we are impatient, give us peace. When we face circumstances that we cannot change, give us a spirit of acceptance. In all things great and small, let us trust in You, Dear Lord, knowing that You are the Giver of life and the Giver of all things good, today and forever. Amen

Chapter 40

Beyond Discouragement

Rejoice in the Lord always.
I will say it again: Rejoice!
Philippians 4:4 HCSB

Christian couples have many reasons to celebrate. God is in His heaven; Christ has risen, and we are the sheep of His flock. Yet sometimes, even the most devout believers may become discouraged. After all, we live in a world where expectations can be high and demands can be even higher.

When we fail to meet the expectations of others (or, for that matter, the expectations that we have for ourselves), we may be tempted to abandon hope. But God has other plans. He knows exactly how He intends to use us. Our task is to remain faithful until He does.

If you or your spouse become discouraged by the direction of life, turn your thoughts and prayers to God. He is a God of possibility, not negativity. He will help you count your blessings instead of your hardships. And then, with a renewed spirit of optimism and hope, you can properly thank your Father in heaven for His blessings, for His love, and for His Son.

To make happiness last, we must obey God while celebrating His blessings. To make happiness disappear, we need only disobey God while ignoring His blessings.

Criswell Freeman

The main joy of heaven will be the Heavenly Father greeting us in a time and place of rejoicing, celebration, joy, and great reunion.

Bill Bright

If you can forgive the person you were, accept the person you are, and believe in the person you will become, you are headed for joy. So celebrate your life.

Barbara Johnson

David and the whole house of Israel were celebrating before the Lord.

2 Samuel 6:5 HCSB

— Our Prayer for Today —

Lord, You are the Giver of all life, and You have created us to have fellowship with You. Let us live our lives in ways that are pleasing to You. We will celebrate together, Father, and we will give thanks for Your blessings today and throughout all eternity. Amen

Chapter 41

How to Start the Day

He awakens Me morning by morning,
He awakens My ear to hear as the learned.
The Lord God has opened My ear.

Isaiah 50:4-5 NKJV

How do you and your spouse prepare for the day ahead? Do you awaken early enough to spend at least a few moments with God? Or do you both sleep until the last possible minute, leaving no time to invest in matters of the heart and soul? Hopefully, you make a habit of spending precious moments each morning with your Creator. When you do, He will fill your hearts, He will direct your thoughts, and He will guide your steps.

Your daily devotional time can be habit-forming, and should be. The first few minutes of each day are invaluable. Treat them that way, and offer them to God.

Maintenance of the devotional mood is indispensable to success in the Christian life.

A. W. Tozer

How motivating it has been for me to view my early morning devotions as time of retreat alone with Jesus, Who desires that I "come with Him by myself to a quiet place" in order to pray, read His Word, listen for His voice, and be renewed in my spirit.

Anne Graham Lotz

Meditating upon His Word will inevitably bring peace of mind, strength of purpose, and power for living.

Bill Bright

It is good to give thanks to the Lord, and to sing praises to Your name, O Most High; to declare Your lovingkindness in the morning, and Your faithfulness every night.

Psalm 92:1-2 NKJV

— Our Prayer for Today —

Dear Lord, to begin the day, we will come to You for guidance, for perspective, for wisdom, and for protection. Today and every day, we will seek to obey Your Word and to honor Your Son. Amen

Chapter 42

Beyond the Doubts

*Now if any of you lacks wisdom, he should ask God,
who gives to all generously and without criticizing,
and it will be given to him. But let him ask in faith
without doubting. For the doubter is like the surging sea,
driven and tossed by the wind.*

James 1:5-6 HCSB

Even the most faithful Christians are overcome by occasional bouts of fear and doubt. You are no different. When you feel that your faith is being tested to its limits, seek the comfort and assurance of the One who sent His Son as a sacrifice for you.

Have you ever felt your faith in God slipping away? If so, you are not alone. Every life—including yours—is a series of successes and failures, celebrations and disappointments, joys and sorrows, hopes and doubts.

But even when you feel very distant from God, remember that God is never distant from you. When you sincerely seek His presence, He will touch your heart, calm your fears, and restore your soul.

In our constant struggle to believe, we are likely to overlook the simple fact that a bit of healthy disbelief is sometimes as needful as faith to the welfare of our souls.

A. W. Tozer

Doubting may temporarily disturb, but will not permanently destroy, your faith in Christ.

Charles Swindoll

Unconfessed sin in your life will cause you to doubt.

Anne Graham Lotz

Immediately the father of the child cried out and said with tears, "Lord, I believe; help my unbelief!"

Mark 9:24 NKJV

— Our Prayer for Today —

Dear Lord, when we are filled with uncertainty and doubt, give us faith. In the dark moments of life, keep us mindful of Your healing power and Your infinite love, so that we may live courageously and faithfully today and every day. Amen

Chapter 43

Your Duties to Him

But as God has distributed to each one,
as the Lord has called each one, so let him walk.

1 Corinthians 7:17 NKJV

Nobody needs to tell you the obvious: You have lots of responsibilities—obligations to yourself, to your mate, to your family, to your community, and to your God. And which of these duties should take priority? The answer can be found in Matthew 6:33: "But seek first the kingdom of God and His righteousness, and all these things will be provided for you" (HCSB).

When you "seek first the kingdom of God," all your other obligations have a way of falling into place. When you obey God's Word and seek His will, your many responsibilities don't seem quite so burdensome. When you honor God with your time, your talents, and your prayers, you'll be much more likely to count your blessings instead of your troubles.

So do yourself and your loved ones a favor: take all your duties seriously, especially your duties to God. When you do, you'll discover that pleasing your Father in heaven isn't just the right thing to do; it's also the best way to live.

If you seek to know the path of your duty, use God as your compass.

C. H. Spurgeon

Discipleship usually brings us into the necessity of choice between duty and desire.

Elisabeth Elliot

When the law of God is written on our hearts, our duty will be our delight.

Matthew Henry

So then each of us shall give account of himself to God.

Romans 14:12 NKJV

— Our Prayer for Today —

Dear Lord, today and every day, let us recognize our responsibilities, and let us fulfill them. And keep us mindful that absolutely no responsibility is greater than our obligation to follow in the footsteps of Your Son. Amen

Chapter 44

Optimistic Christianity

But if we hope for what we do not see,
we eagerly wait for it with patience.

Romans 8:25 HCSB

Pessimism and Christianity don't mix. Why? Because Christians have every reason to be optimistic about life here on earth and life eternal. As C. H. Spurgeon observed, "Our hope in Christ for the future is the mainstream of our joy." But sometimes, we fall prey to worry, frustration, anxiety, or sheer exhaustion, and our hearts become heavy. What's needed is plenty of rest, a large dose of perspective, and God's healing touch, but not necessarily in that order.

Today, make this promise to yourself and keep it: vow to be a hope-filled Christian. Think optimistically about your life, your profession, your future, and your spouse. Trust your hopes, not your fears. Take time to celebrate God's glorious creation. And then, when you've filled your heart with hope and gladness, share your optimism with others. They'll be better for it, and so will you. But not necessarily in that order.

Keep your feet on the ground, but let your heart soar as high as it will. Refuse to be average or to surrender to the chill of your spiritual environment.

A. W. Tozer

The Christian lifestyle is not one of legalistic do's and don'ts, but one that is positive, attractive, and joyful.

Vonette Bright

Christ can put a spring in your step and a thrill in your heart. Optimism and cheerfulness are products of knowing Christ.

Billy Graham

Make me hear joy and gladness.

Psalm 51:8 NKJV

— Our Prayer for Today —

Thank You, Lord, for Your infinite love. Make us both optimistic Christians, Father, as we place our hopes and our trust in You. Amen

Chapter 45

Parents Shape Eternity

Train up a child in the way he should go:
and when he is old, he will not depart from it.

Proverbs 22:6 KJV

I f you're parents in our 21st-century world, you need keen insight, prudent foresight, and sharp eyesight. But that's not all. You also need discipline, patience, prayer, and a willingness to teach.

Parents are their kids' most important instructors. Daniel Webster wrote, "If we work in marble, it will perish; if we work upon brass, time will efface it; if we rear temples, they will crumble into dust; but if we work upon immortal minds and instill in them just principles, we are then engraving upon tablets which no time will efface, but which will brighten and brighten to all eternity." These words remind us of the glorious opportunities that are available to those of us who teach our children well.

Are you and your spouse teaching from the same curriculum? And does that curriculum begin and end with The Book? Hopefully so, because that's exactly what your children need.

Do you sincerely seek to leave a lasting legacy for generations to come? If so, you must start by teaching your children the ways and the Word of God. And remember always that your most enduring lessons are not the ones you teach with words; they are the ones you teach by example. When you obey God's commandments and trust His promises, your life will be a shining lesson for your children . . . and for theirs.

Kids aren't looking for perfect parents, but they are looking for honest and growing ones.

Howard Hendricks

If it is important to produce respectful, responsible young citizens, then we should set out to mold them accordingly.

James Dobson

Parents, don't come down too hard on your children or you'll crush their spirits.

Colossians 3:21 MSG

— Our Prayer for Today —

Dear Lord, help us be responsible, loving, godly parents. Let us teach our children to worship You and to study Your Word. When we are uncertain, Lord, give us wisdom. And, in everything that we do and say, let us be worthy examples to our family members every day that we live. Amen

Chapter 46

He Leads

However, I did give them this command:
Obey Me, and then I will be your God,
and you will be My people. You must walk
in every way I command you so that
it may go well with you.

Jeremiah 7:23 HCSB

When we genuinely open our hearts to God, He speaks to us through a small, still voice within. When He does, we can listen, or not. When we pay careful attention to the Father, He leads us along a path of His choosing, a path that leads to abundance, peace, joy, and eternal life. But when we choose to ignore God, we select a path that is not His, and we must endure the consequences of our shortsightedness.

Today, focus your thoughts and your prayers on the path that God intends for you to take. When you do, your loving Heavenly Father will speak to your heart. When He does, listen carefully . . . and trust Him.

Only by walking with God can we hope to find the path that leads to life.

John Eldredge

It is God to whom and with whom we travel, while He is the End of our journey, He is also at every stopping place.

Elisabeth Elliot

When we truly walk with God throughout our day, life slowly starts to fall into place.

Bill Hybels

Trust in the Lord with all your heart, and lean not on your own understanding; In all your ways acknowledge Him, and He shall direct your paths.

Proverbs 3:5-6 NKJV

— Our Prayer for Today —

Dear Lord, help us find the path that You intend for us to follow. We can live courageously, Father, because we know that You are leading us to a place of Your choosing . . . and where You lead, we will follow. Amen

Chapter 47

Built upon Trust

Those who trust in the Lord are like Mount Zion.
It cannot be shaken; it remains forever.

Psalm 125:1 HCSB

The best relationships—and the best marriages—are built upon a foundation of honesty and trust. Without trust, marriages soon begin to wither; with trust, marriages soon begin to flourish.

For Christians, honesty is the right policy because it's God's policy. God's Word makes it clear: "Lying lips are an abomination to the Lord, but those who deal truthfully are His delight" (Proverbs 12:22 NKJV).

Sometimes, honesty is difficult; sometimes, honesty is painful; sometimes, honesty makes us feel uncomfortable. Despite these temporary feelings of discomfort, we must make honesty the hallmark of all our relationships; otherwise, we invite needless suffering into our own lives and into the lives of those we love.

Do you want your love to last forever? Then you and your spouse must commit to build a relationship based upon mutual trust and unerring truth. Both of you deserve nothing less . . . and neither, for that matter, does God.

Trust is like "money in the bank" in a marriage. There must be a reasonable amount of it on deposit to ensure the security of a marital union.

Ed Young

How committed are you to breaking the ice of prayerlessness so that you and your mate can seek the Lord openly and honestly together, releasing control over your marriage into the capable, trustworthy, but often surprising hands of God?

Stormie Omartian

Two words will help you cope when you run low on hope: accept and trust.

Charles Swindoll

For in it God's righteousness is revealed from faith to faith, just as it is written: The righteous will live by faith.

Romans 1:17 HCSB

— Our Prayer for Today —

Dear Lord, as we build our marriage day by day, we will build it upon trust—trust in each other and trust in You. Amen

Whom to Please?

For am I now trying to win the favor of people, or God?
Or am I striving to please people?
If I were still trying to please people,
I would not be a slave of Christ.

Galatians 1:10 HCSB

R ick Warren observed, "Those who follow the crowd usually get lost in it." We know these words to be true, but oftentimes we fail to live by them. Instead of trusting God for guidance, we imitate our neighbors and suffer the consequences. Instead of seeking to please our Father in heaven, we strive to please our peers, with decidedly mixed results.

Whom will you both try to please today: your God or your friends? Your obligation is most certainly not to neighbors, to friends, or even to family members. Your obligation is to an all-knowing, all-powerful God. You must seek to please Him first and always. No exceptions.

You must never sacrifice your relationship with God for the sake of a relationship with another person.

Charles Stanley

Many people never receive God's best for them because they are addicted to the approval of others.

Joyce Meyer

Blessed is the man who walks not in the counsel of the ungodly, nor stands in the path of sinners, nor sits in the seat of the scornful; but his delight is in the law of the Lord, and in His law he meditates day and night.

Psalm 1:1-2 NKJV

— Our Prayer for Today —

Dear Lord, today we will worry less about pleasing other people and more about pleasing You. We will honor You with our thoughts, our actions, and our prayers. And we will worship You, Father, with thanksgiving in our hearts, this day and forever. Amen

Perspective for Today

Make me to hear joy and gladness. . . .
Psalm 51:8 KJV

I f a temporary loss of perspective has left you worried, exhausted, or both, it's time to readjust your thought patterns. Negative thoughts are habit-forming; thankfully, so are positive ones. With practice, you can form the habit of focusing on God's priorities and your own possibilities. When you do, you'll soon discover that you will spend less time fretting about your challenges and more time praising God for His gifts.

When you call upon the Lord and prayerfully seek His will, He will give you wisdom and perspective. When you make God's priorities your priorities, He will direct your steps and calm your fears. So today and every day hereafter, pray for a sense of balance and perspective. And remember: no problems are too big for God—and that includes yours.

Instead of being frustrated and overwhelmed by all that is going on in our world, go to the Lord and ask Him to give you His eternal perspective.

Kay Arthur

The proper perspective creates within us a spirit of reaching outside of ourselves with joy and enthusiasm.

Luci Swindoll

Earthly fears are no fears at all. Answer the big questions of eternity, and the little questions of life fall into perspective.

Max Lucado

My cup runs over. Surely goodness and mercy shall follow me all the days of my life; and I will dwell in the house of the Lord Forever.

Psalm 23:5-6 NKJV

— Our Prayer for Today —

Dear Lord, sometimes, the world's perspective can lead us astray. Give us guidance, wisdom, and perspective. And keep us mindful, Father, that Your reality is the ultimate reality, and that Your truth is the ultimate truth, now and forever. Amen

Chapter 50

When the Answer Is No

Can you search out the deep things of God?
Can you find out the limits of the Almighty?
They are higher than heaven—what can you do?
Deeper than Sheol—what can you know?
Their measure is longer than the earth
And broader than the sea.

Job 11:7-9 NKJV

God answers our prayers. What God does not do is this: He does not always answer our prayers as soon as we might like, and He does not always answer our prayers by saying "Yes." God isn't an order-taker, and He's not some sort of cosmic vending machine. Sometimes—even when we want something very badly—our loving Heavenly Father responds to our requests by saying "No," and we must accept His answer, even if we don't understand it.

God answers prayers not only according to our wishes but also according to His master plan. We cannot know that plan, but we can know the Planner . . . and we must trust His wisdom, His righteousness, and His love. Always.

If God chooses to remain silent, faith is content.

Ruth Bell Graham

He who kneels most stands best.

D. L. Moody

The story of every great Christian achievement is the history of answered prayer.

E. M. Bounds

For now we see indistinctly, as in a mirror, but then face to face. Now I know in part, but then I will know fully, as I am fully known.

1 Corinthians 13:12 HCSB

— Our Prayer for Today —

We pray to You, Father, because You desire it and because we need it. Prayer not only changes things; it changes us. Help us, Lord, never to face the demands of the day without first spending time with You. Amen

Chapter 51

Purposeful Living

Whatever you do, do all to the glory of God.

1 Corinthians 10:31 NKJV

Each morning, as the sun rises in the east, you both welcome a new day, a day that is filled to the brim with opportunities, with possibilities, and with God. As you contemplate God's blessings in your own lives, you should prayerfully seek His guidance for the day ahead.

Discovering God's unfolding purpose for your marriage is a daily journey, a journey guided by the teachings of God's Holy Word. As you reflect upon God's promises and upon the meaning that those promises hold for each of you, ask God to lead you throughout the coming day. Let your Heavenly Father direct your steps; concentrate on what God wants you to do now, and leave the distant future in hands that are far more capable than your own: His hands.

The Christian life is not simply following principles but being empowered to fulfill our purpose: knowing and exalting Christ.

Franklin Graham

It is important to set goals because if you do not have a plan, a goal, a direction, a purpose, and a focus, you are not going to accomplish anything for the glory of God.

Bill Bright

How much of our lives are, well, so daily. How often our hours are filled with the mundane, seemingly unimportant things that have to be done, whether at home or work. These very "daily" tasks could become a celebration of praise. "It is through consecration," someone has said, "that drudgery is made divine."

Gigi Graham Tchividjian

In Him we were also made His inheritance, predestined according to the purpose of the One who works out everything in agreement with the decision of His will.

Ephesians 1:11 HCSB

— Our Prayer for Today —

Dear Lord, You are the Creator of the universe, and we know that Your plan for our lives is grander than we can imagine. Let Your purposes be our purposes, and let us trust in the assurance of Your promises. Amen

Chapter 52

Questions?

*We are pressured in every way but not crushed;
we are perplexed but not in despair.*

2 Corinthians 4:8 HCSB

When you have a question that you simply can't answer, whom do you ask? When you face a difficult decision, to whom do you turn for counsel? To friends? To mentors? To family members? Or do you turn first to the ultimate source of wisdom? The answers to life's big questions start with God and with the teachings of His Holy Word.

God's wisdom stands forever. God's Word is a light for every generation. Make it your light as well. Use the Bible as a compass for the next stage of your life's journey. Use it as the yardstick by which your behavior is measured. And as you carefully consult the pages of God's Word, prayerfully ask Him to reveal the wisdom that you need. When you take your concerns to God, He will not turn you away; He will, instead, offer answers that are tested and true. Your job is to ask, to listen, and to trust.

Be to the world a sign that while we as Christians do not have all the answers, we do know and care about the questions.

Billy Graham

We are finding we don't have such a gnawing need to know the answers when we know the Answer.

Gloria Gaither

When there is perplexity there is always guidance—not always at the moment we ask, but in good time, which is God's time. There is no need to fret and stew.

Elisabeth Elliot

Come to terms with God and be at peace; in this way good will come to you.

Job 22:21 HCSB

— Our Prayer for Today —

Dear God, sometimes this world can be a puzzling place. When we are unsure of our next steps, keep us aware that You are always near. Give us faith, Father, and let us remember that with Your love and Your power, we can live courageously and faithfully today and every day. Amen

Chapter 53

Renewal

*I will give you a new heart
and put a new spirit within you.*

Ezekiel 36:26 NKJV

When we genuinely lift our hearts and prayers to God, He renews our strength. Are you almost too weary to lift your head? Then bow it. Offer your concerns and your fears to your Father in heaven. He is always at your side, offering His love and His strength.

Are either of you troubled or anxious? Take your anxieties to God in prayer. Are you weak or worried? Delve deeply into God's Holy Word and sense His presence in the quiet moments of the early morning. Are you spiritually exhausted? Call upon fellow believers to support you, and call upon Christ to renew your spirit and your life. Your Savior will never let you down. To the contrary, He will always lift you up if you ask Him to. So what, dear friends, are you waiting for?

One reason so much American Christianity is a mile wide and an inch deep is that Christians are simply tired. Sometimes you need to kick back and rest for Jesus' sake.

Dennis Swanberg

God specializes in things fresh and firsthand. His plans for you this year may outshine those of the past. He's prepared to fill your days with reasons to give Him praise.

Joni Eareckson Tada

Father, for this day, renew within me the gift of the Holy Spirit.

Andrew Murray

In the multitude of my anxieties within me, Your comforts delight my soul.

Psalm 94:19 NKJV

— Our Prayer for Today —

Heavenly Father, sometimes we are troubled, and sometimes we grow weary. When we are weak, Lord, give us strength. When we are discouraged, renew us. When we are fearful, let us feel Your healing touch. Let us always trust in Your promises, Lord, and let us draw strength from those promises and from Your unending love. Amen

Chapter 54

Be Still

Be silent before the Lord
and wait expectantly for Him.
Psalm 37:7 HCSB

Ours is a fast-paced world. The demands of the day can seem overwhelming at times, but when we slow ourselves down and seek the presence of a loving God, we invite His peace into our hearts.

Do you carve out quiet moments each day to offer thanksgiving and praise to your Creator? You should. During these moments of stillness, you will often sense the infinite love and power of our Lord.

The familiar words of Psalm 46:10 remind us to "be still, and know that I am God." When we do so, we encounter the awesome presence of our loving Heavenly Father, and we are blessed beyond words.

We can seek God and find him! God is knowable, touchable, hearable, seeable, with the mind, the hands, the ears, and eyes of the inner man.

A. W. Tozer

Man was created by God to know and love Him in a permanent, personal relationship.

Anne Graham Lotz

Let your loneliness be transformed into a holy aloneness. Sit still before the Lord. Remember Naomi's word to Ruth: "Sit still, my daughter, until you see how the matter will fall."

Elisabeth Elliot

Be still, and know that I am God. . . .

Psalm 46:10 KJV

— Our Prayer for Today —

Dear Lord, let us be still before You. When we are hurried or distracted, slow us down and redirect our thoughts. When we are confused, give us perspective. Keep us mindful, Father, that You are always with us. And let us sense Your presence now and forever. Amen

Chapter 55

Beyond Guilt

Blessed is the man who does not condemn himself.
Romans 14:22 HCSB

All of us have sinned. Sometimes our sins result from our own stubborn rebellion against God's commandments. And sometimes, we are swept up in events that are beyond our abilities to control. Under either set of circumstances, we may experience intense feelings of guilt. But God has an answer for the guilt that we feel. That answer, of course, is His forgiveness. When we confess our wrongdoings and repent from them, we are forgiven by the One who created us.

Are you troubled by feelings of guilt or regret? If so, you must repent from your misdeeds, and you must ask your Heavenly Father for His forgiveness. When you do so, He will forgive you completely and without reservation. Then, you must forgive yourself just as God has forgiven you: thoroughly and unconditionally.

Satan wants you to feel guilty. Your heavenly Father wants you to know that you are forgiven.

Warren Wiersbe

Let's take Jesus at this word. When he says we're forgiven, let's unload the guilt. When he says we're valuable, let's believe him. When he says we're eternal, let's bury our fear. When he says we're provided for, let's stop worrying.

Max Lucado

Don't be bound by your guilt or your fears any longer, but realize that sin's penalty has already been paid by Christ completely and fully.

Billy Graham

There is therefore now no condemnation to those who are in Christ Jesus, who do not walk according to the flesh, but according to the Spirit.

Romans 8:1 NKJV

— Our Prayer for Today —

Dear Lord, thank You for the guilt that we feel when we disobey You. Help us confess our wrongdoings, help us accept Your forgiveness, and help us renew our passion to serve You. Amen

Habits Matter

Do not be deceived:
"Evil company corrupts good habits."
1 Corinthians 15:33 NKJV

It's an old saying and a true one: First, you make your habits, and then your habits make you. Some habits will inevitably bring you closer to God; other habits will lead you away from the path He has chosen for you. If you sincerely desire to improve your spiritual health, you must honestly examine the habits that make up the fabric of your day. And you must abandon those habits that are displeasing to God.

If you trust God, and if you keep asking for His help, He can transform your life. If you sincerely ask Him to help you, the same God who created the universe will help you defeat the harmful habits that have heretofore defeated you. So, if at first you don't succeed, keep praying. God is listening, and He's ready to help you become a better person if you ask Him . . . so ask today.

The simple fact is that if we sow a lifestyle that is in direct disobedience to God's revealed Word, we ultimately reap disaster.

Charles Swindoll

Since behaviors become habits, make them work with you and not against you.

E. Stanley Jones

You will never change your life until you change something you do daily.

John Maxwell

Teach me to do Your will, for You are my God; Your Spirit is good. Lead me in the land of uprightness.

Psalm 143:10 NKJV

— Our Prayer for Today —

Dear Lord, help us break bad habits and form good ones. And let our actions be pleasing to You, today and every day. Amen

Chapter 57

He Is Sufficient

The Lord is my strength and my song;
He has become my salvation.

Exodus 15:2 HCSB

It is easy to become overwhelmed by the demands of everyday life, but if you're a faithful follower of the One from Galilee, you need never be overwhelmed. Why? Because God's love is sufficient to meet your needs. Whatever dangers you both may face, whatever heartbreaks you must endure, God is with you, and He stands ready to comfort you and to heal you.

The Psalmist writes, "Weeping may endure for a night, but joy comes in the morning" (Psalm 30:5 NKJV). But when we are suffering, the morning may seem very far away. It is not. God promises that He is "near to those who have a broken heart" (Psalm 34:18 NKJV).

If you are experiencing the intense pain of a recent loss, or if you are still mourning a loss from long ago, perhaps you are now ready to begin the next stage of your journey with God. If so, be mindful of this fact: the loving heart of God is sufficient to meet any challenge, including yours.

God is always sufficient in perfect proportion to our need.

Beth Moore

God is, must be, our answer to every question and every cry of need.

Hannah Whitall Smith

God's all-sufficiency is a major. Your inability is a minor. Major in majors, not in minors.

Corrie ten Boom

Finally, my brethren, be strong in the Lord and in the power of His might. Put on the whole armor of God, that you may be able to stand against the wiles of the devil.

Ephesians 6:10-11 NKJV

— Our Prayer for Today —

Dear Lord, whatever "it" is, You can handle it! Let us turn to You when we are fearful or worried. You are our loving Heavenly Father; You are sufficient in all things; and we trust You always. Amen

Chapter 58

Enough Rest?

*And the apostles gathered themselves together unto Jesus,
and told him all things, both what they had done,
and what they had taught. And he said unto them, Come
ye yourselves apart into a desert place, and rest a while.*

Mark 6:30-31 HCSB

Even the most inspired Christians can, from time to time, find themselves running on empty. The demands of daily life can drain us of our strength and rob us of the joy that is rightfully ours in Christ. When we find ourselves tired, discouraged, or worse, there is a source from which we can draw the power needed to recharge our spiritual batteries. That source is God.

God intends that His children lead joyous lives filled with abundance and peace. But sometimes, abundance and peace seem very far away. It is then that we must turn to God for renewal, and when we do, He will restore us.

God expects us to work hard, but He also intends for us to rest. When we fail to take the rest that we need, we do a disservice to ourselves and to our families.

Are your spiritual batteries running low? Is your energy on the wane? Are your emotions frayed? If so, it's time to turn your thoughts and your prayers to God. And when you're finished, it's time to rest.

Notice what Jesus had to say concerning those who have wearied themselves by trying to do things in their own strength: "Come to me, all you who labor and are heavy laden, and I will give you rest."

Henry Blackaby and Claude King

Some of us would do more for the Lord if we did less.

Vance Havner

Thou hast formed us for Thyself, and our hearts are restless till they find rest in Thee.

St. Augustine

Come to Me, all you who labor and are heavy laden, and I will give you rest. Take My yoke upon you and learn from Me, for I am gentle and lowly in heart, and you will find rest for your souls. For My yoke is easy and My burden is light.

Matthew 11:28-30 NKJV

— Our Prayer for Today —

Dear Lord, when we're tired, give us the wisdom to do the smart thing: give us the wisdom to rest. Amen

Chapter 59

Accepting His Love

God is love, and the one who remains in love remains in God, and God remains in him.

1 John 4:16 HCSB

God loves our world. He loves it so much, in fact, that He sent His only begotten Son to die for our sins. And now we, as believers, are challenged to return God's love by obeying His commandments and honoring His Son.

When you and your spouse allow Christ to reign over your lives and your marriage, you will be transformed: you will feel differently about yourselves, your marriage, your family, and your world. When you and your beloved feel God's presence and invite His Son to rule your hearts and your household, your family will be eternally blessed.

God loved this world so much that He sent His Son to save it. And now only one real question remains: what will you and yours do in response to God's love? The answer should be obvious: If you haven't already done so, accept Jesus Christ as your Savior. He's waiting patiently for you, but please don't make Him wait another minute longer.

If God had a refrigerator, your picture would be on it. If he had a wallet, your photo would be in it. He sends you flowers every spring and a sunrise every morning.

Max Lucado

Love has its source in God, for love is the very essence of His being.

Kay Arthur

Joy comes from knowing God loves me and knows who I am and where I'm going . . . that my future is secure as I rest in Him.

James Dobson

As the Father loved Me, I also have loved you; abide in My love.

John 15:9 NKJV

—— Our Prayer for Today ——

Thank You, Lord, for Your love. Your love is boundless, infinite, and eternal. Today, we will pause and reflect upon Your love for us, and we will share that love with the people who cross our paths. And, as an expression of our love for You, Father, we will share the saving message of Your Son with a world in desperate need of His peace. Amen

Chapter 60

Using Your Talents

As each one has received a gift,
minister it to one another,
as good stewards of the manifold grace of God.
1 Peter 4:10 NKJV

The old saying is both familiar and true: "What we are is God's gift to us; what we become is our gift to God." Each of us possesses special talents, gifted by God, that can be nurtured carefully or ignored totally. Our challenge, of course, is to use our abilities to the greatest extent possible and to use them in ways that honor our Savior.

Are you both using your natural talents to make God's world a better place? If so, congratulations. But if you have gifts that you have not fully explored and developed, perhaps you need to have a chat with the One who gave you those gifts in the first place. Your talents are priceless treasures offered from your Heavenly Father. Use them. After all, an obvious way to say "thank You" to the Giver is to use the gifts He has given.

God has given you special talents—now it's your turn to give them back to God.

Marie T. Freeman

If you want to reach your potential, you need to add a strong work ethic to your talent.

John Maxwell

You are the only person on earth who can use your ability.

Zig Ziglar

Do not neglect the gift that is in you.

1 Timothy 4:14 HCSB

— Our Prayer for Today —

Dear Lord, You have given us talents, and we thank You. Today, we will be good and faithful stewards of our talents, our possessions, and our opportunities. We will share our gifts with the world, and we will offer praise to You, the Giver of all things good. Amen

Chapter 61

Managing Time

There is an occasion for everything,
and a time for every activity under heaven.
Ecclesiastes 3:1 HCSB

Time is a nonrenewable gift from God. But sometimes, we treat our time here on earth as if it were not a gift at all: We may be tempted to invest our lives in trivial pursuits and petty diversions. But our Father beckons each of us to a higher calling.

An important element of our stewardship to God is the way that we choose to spend the time He has entrusted to us. Each waking moment holds the potential to do a good deed, to say a kind word, or to offer a heartfelt prayer. Our challenge, as believers, is to use our time wisely in the service of God's work and in accordance with His plan for our lives.

Each day is a special treasure to be savored and celebrated. May we—as Christians who have so much to celebrate—never fail to praise our Creator by rejoicing in this glorious day, and by using it wisely.

God has a present will for your life. It is neither chaotic nor utterly exhausting. In the midst of many good choices vying for your time, He will give you the discernment to recognize what is best.

Beth Moore

Our leisure, even our play, is a matter of serious concern. There is no neutral ground in the universe: every square inch, every split second, is claimed by God and counterclaimed by Satan.

C. S. Lewis

We can't afford to waste a minute, must not squander these precious daylight hours in frivolity and indulgence, in sleeping around and dissipation, in bickering and grabbing everything in sight. Get out of bed and get dressed! Don't loiter and linger, waiting until the very last minute. Dress yourselves in Christ, and be up and about!

Romans 13:13-14 MSG

— Our Prayer for Today —

Dear Lord, You have given us a wonderful gift: time together here on earth. Let us use it wisely—for the glory of Your kingdom and the betterment of Your world—today and every day. Amen

Chapter 62

Still Learning

I will instruct you and teach you
in the way you should go;
I will guide you with My eye.
Psalm 32:8 NKJV

Whether you're twenty-two or a hundred and two, you've still got lots to learn. Even if you're a very wise person, God isn't finished with you yet. Why? Because lifetime learning is part of God's plan—and He certainly hasn't finished teaching you some very important lessons.

Do you seek to live a life of righteousness and wisdom? If so, you must continue to study the ultimate source of wisdom: the Word of God. You must associate, day in and day out, with godly men and women. And, you must act in accordance with your beliefs. When you study God's Word and live according to His commandments, you will become wise . . . and you will be a blessing to your friends, to your family, and to the world.

The essence of wisdom, from a practical standpoint, is pausing long enough to look at our lives—invitations, opportunities, relationships—from God's perspective. And then acting on it.

Charles Stanley

God does not give His counsel to the curious or the careless; He reveals His will to the concerned and to the consecrated.

Warren Wiersbe

The fruit of wisdom is Christlikeness, peace, humility, and love. And, the root of it is faith in Christ as the manifested wisdom of God.

J. I. Packer

Wisdom is the principal thing; therefore get wisdom. And in all your getting, get understanding.

Proverbs 4:7 NKJV

— Our Prayer for Today —

We seek wisdom, Lord, not as the world gives, but as You give. Lead us in Your ways and teach us from Your Word so that, in time, our wisdom might glorify Your kingdom and Your Son. Amen

Chapter 63

Beyond Worry

So don't worry, saying, "What will we eat?" or
"What will we drink?" or "What will we wear?"
For the Gentiles eagerly seek all these things, and your
heavenly Father knows that you need them. But seek first
the kingdom of God and His righteousness, and all these
things will be provided for you. Therefore don't worry
about tomorrow, because tomorrow will worry about
itself. Each day has enough trouble of its own.

Matthew 6:31-34 HCSB

Because we are imperfect human beings struggling with imperfect circumstances, we worry. Even though we, as Christians, have the assurance of salvation—even though we, as Christians, have the promise of God's love and protection—we find ourselves fretting over the inevitable frustrations of everyday life (not to mention married life). Jesus understood our concerns when He spoke the reassuring words found in the 6th chapter of Matthew.

Where is the best place to take your worries? Take them to God. Take your troubles to Him; take your fears to Him; take your doubts to Him; take your weaknesses to Him; take your sorrows to Him . . . and leave them all there. Seek protection from the One who offers you eternal salvation; build your spiritual house upon the Rock that cannot be moved.

Perhaps you are concerned about your family, your future, your health, or your finances. Or perhaps you are simply a "worrier" by nature. If so, make Matthew 6 a regular part of your daily Bible reading. This beautiful passage will remind you that God still sits in His heaven and you are His beloved child. Then, perhaps, you will worry a little less and trust God a little more, and that's as it should be because God is trustworthy . . . and you are protected.

Today is the tomorrow we worried about yesterday.

Dennis Swanberg

When I am filled with cares, Your comfort brings me joy.

Psalm 94:19 HCSB

— Our Prayer for Today —

Dear Lord, You understand our worries and our fears—and You forgive us when we are weak. When our faith begins to waver, Father, help us to trust You more. Then, with Your Holy Word on our lips and with the love of Your Son in our hearts, let us live courageously, faithfully, prayerfully, and thankfully today and every day. Amen

Chapter 64

The Media's Messages

*Let no one deceive himself. If anyone among you seems
to be wise in this age, let him become a fool that he may
become wise. For the wisdom of this world is
foolishness with God. For it is written,
"He catches the wise in their own craftiness."*

1 Corinthians 3:18–19 NKJV

I f you and your loved ones have acquired the bad
habit of watching whatever happens to pop up on
your family's TV screen, it's time to rethink the
way you control your clicker. Most television networks
(as well as the other forms of popular media) can be
dangerous to your emotional and spiritual health.

The media is working around the clock in an
attempt to rearrange your family's priorities in ways
that are definitely not in your best interests. The media
is trying to teach your family that physical appearance
is all-important, that material possessions should
be acquired at any cost, and that the world operates
independently of God's laws. But guess what? Those
messages are lies.

In the pursuit of profits, the media glamorizes
violence, exploits suffering, and sensationalizes sex, all
in the name of "ratings" (translated: "money").

So here's a question for you and your family: Will
you control what appears on your TV screen, or will you

be controlled by it? If you're willing to take complete control over the images that appear inside the four walls of your home, you'll be doing yourselves a king-sized favor. So forget the media hype, and pay attention to God. Stand up for Him and be counted, not just in church where it's relatively easy to be a Christian, but also when you're deciding what to watch. You owe it to your Creator . . . and you owe it to yourselves.

The only ultimate disaster that can befall us, I have come to realize, is to feel ourselves to be home on earth.

Max Lucado

Do not love the world or the things in the world. If anyone loves the world, the love of the Father is not in him.

1 John 2:15 NKJV

— Our Prayer for Today —

Lord, this world is filled with temptations and distractions; we have many opportunities to stray from Your commandments. Help us to focus not on the things of this world, but on the message of Your Son. Let us keep Christ in our hearts as we follow Him this day and forever. Amen

Chapter 65

Miracles

But He said, "The things which are impossible
with men are possible with God."
Luke 18:27 NKJV

D o you both believe in an all-powerful God who can do miraculous things in you and through you? You should. But perhaps, as you have faced the inevitable struggles of life here on earth, you have—without realizing it—placed limitations on God. To do so is a profound mistake. God's power has no such limitations, and He can work mighty miracles in your own life if you let Him.

Do you lack a firm faith in God's power to perform miracles for you and your loved ones? If so, you are attempting to place constraints on a God who has none. So instead of doubting your Heavenly Father, place yourself in His hands. Instead of doubting God's power, you must trust it. Expect Him to work miracles, and be watchful. With God, absolutely nothing is impossible, including an amazing assortment of miracles that He stands ready, willing, and perfectly able to perform for you and yours.

We have a God who delights in impossibilities.

Andrew Murray

The miracles in fact are a retelling in small letters of the very same story which is written across the whole world in letters too large for some of us to see.

C. S. Lewis

When God is involved, anything can happen. Be open and stay that way. God has a beautiful way of bringing good vibrations out of broken chords.

Charles Swindoll

But as it is written: "Eye has not seen, nor ear heard, nor have entered into the heart of man the things which God has prepared for those who love Him."

1 Corinthians 2:9 NKJV

— Our Prayer for Today —

Heavenly Father, Your infinite power is beyond human understanding. With You nothing is impossible. Keep us mindful of Your power, and let us share the glorious message of Your miracles. When we lose hope, give us faith; when others lose hope, let us tell them of Your glory and Your works. Today, Lord, let us expect the miraculous, let us praise You, and let us give thanks for Your miracles. Amen

Chapter 66

Arguments Lost

But stay away from those who have foolish arguments
and talk about useless family histories and argue
and quarrel about the law. Those things are worth
nothing and will not help anyone.

Titus 3:9 NCV

A rguments are seldom won but often lost. When we engage in petty squabbles, our losses usually outpace our gains. When we acquire the unfortunate habit of habitual bickering, we do harm to our spouses, to our families, to our friends, to our coworkers, and to ourselves.

Time and again, God's Word warns us that most arguments are a monumental waste of time, of energy, of life. In Titus 3:9, we are warned to refrain from "foolish arguments," and with good reason. Such arguments usually do more for the devil than they do for God.

So the next time you're tempted to engage in a silly squabble, whether inside the church or outside it, refrain. When you do, you'll put a smile on God's face, and you'll send the devil packing.

Some fights are lost even though we win. A bulldog can whip a skunk, but it just isn't worth it.

Vance Havner

The Gospel has to be experienced, not argued!

Grady Nutt

Whatever you do when conflicts arise, be wise. Fight against jumping to quick conclusions and seeing only your side. There are always two sides on the streets of conflict. Look both ways.

Charles Swindoll

I tell you that on the day of judgment people will have to account for every careless word they speak. For by your words you will be acquitted, and by your words you will be condemned.

Matthew 12:36-37 HCSB

— Our Prayer for Today —

Dear Lord, when we are tempted to be argumentative, keep us calm. When we fall prey to pettiness, restore our sense of perspective. When we are gripped by irrational anger, give us serenity. Let us show our thankfulness to You by offering forgiveness to others. And, when we do, may others see Your love reflected in our words and our deeds. Amen

Chapter 67

Strengthening Your Faith . . . and Your Marriage

Watch, stand fast in the faith, be brave, be strong.
1 Corinthians 16:13 NKJV

Would you and your spouse like to strengthen the bonds of your marriage? Here's a wonderful place to start: by strengthening your faith in God.

Every life and every marriage is a series of successes and failures, celebrations and disappointments, joys and sorrows. Every step of the way, through every triumph and tragedy, God will stand by your side and strengthen you . . . if you have faith in Him. Jesus taught His disciples that if they had faith, they could move mountains. You can too.

When a suffering woman sought healing by merely touching the hem of His cloak, Jesus replied, "Daughter, be of good comfort; thy faith hath made thee whole" (Matthew 9:22 KJV). The message to believers of every generation is clear: we must live by faith today and every day.

When you and your spouse place your faith, your trust, indeed your life in the hands of Christ Jesus, you'll be amazed at the marvelous things He can do with you and through you. So strengthen your faith and your marriage through praise, through worship, through Bible study, and through prayer. And trust God's plans. With Him, all things are possible, and He stands ready to open a world of possibilities to you and yours . . . if you have faith.

Forgive us our lack of faith, lest ulcers become our badge of disbelief.

Peter Marshall

Faith in faith is pointless. Faith in a living, active God moves mountains.

Beth Moore

For whatever is born of God overcomes the world. And this is the victory that has overcome the world—our faith.

1 John 5:4 NKJV

— Our Prayer for Today —

Dear Lord, keep us mindful that You are always near and that You can overcome any challenge. With Your love and Your power, Father, we can live courageously and faithfully today and every day. Amen

Chapter 68

Character Counts

Do not be deceived:
"Bad company corrupts good morals."
1 Corinthians 15:33 HCSB

B eth Moore correctly observed, "Those who walk in truth walk in liberty." Godly husbands and wives agree. As believers in Christ, we must seek to live each day with discipline, honesty, and faith. When we do, at least two things happen: integrity becomes a habit, and God blesses us because of our obedience to Him. Living a life of integrity isn't always the easiest way, but it is always the right way . . . and God clearly intends that it should be our way, too.

Character isn't built overnight; it is built slowly over a lifetime. It is the sum of every sensible choice, every honorable decision, and every honest word. It is forged on the anvil of sincerity and polished by the virtue of fairness. Character is a precious thing—preserve yours at all costs.

Let God use times of waiting to mold and shape your character. Let God use those times to purify your life and make you into a clean vessel for His service.

Henry Blackaby and Claude King

Often, our character is at greater risk in prosperity than in adversity.

Beth Moore

Your true character is something that no one can injure but yourself.

C. H. Spurgeon

But also for this very reason, giving all diligence, add to your faith virtue, to virtue knowledge.

2 Peter 1:5 NKJV

— Our Prayer for Today —

Lord, You know us far better than we know ourselves. Today, we will strive to serve You and to obey Your commandments. Let our words and deeds be pleasing to You this day and every day. Amen

Chapter 69

So Many Choices

I have set before you life and death, blessing and curse.
Choose life so that you and your descendants may live,
love the Lord your God, obey Him, and remain faithful
to Him. For He is your life, and He will prolong
your life in the land the Lord swore to give to
your fathers Abraham, Isaac, and Jacob.

Deuteronomy 30:19-20 HCSB

Because we are creatures of free will, we make choices—lots of them. When we make choices that are pleasing to our Heavenly Father, we are blessed. When we make choices that cause us to walk in the footsteps of God's Son, we enjoy the abundance that Christ has promised to those who follow Him. But when we make choices that are displeasing to God, we sow seeds that have the potential to bring forth a bitter harvest.

Today, as you both encounter the challenges of everyday living, you will make hundreds of choices. Choose wisely. Make your thoughts and your actions pleasing to God. And remember: every choice that is displeasing to Him is the wrong choice—no exceptions.

Many jokes are made about the devil, but the devil is no joke. He is called a deceiver. In order to accomplish his purpose, the devil blinds people to their need for Christ. Two forces are at work in our world—the forces of Christ and the forces of the devil—and you are asked to choose.

Billy Graham

Life is pretty much like a cafeteria line—it offers us many choices, both good and bad. The Christian must have a spiritual radar that detects the difference not only between bad and good but also among good, better, and best.

Dennis Swanberg

Faith is not a feeling; it is action. It is a willed choice.

Elisabeth Elliot

A house is built by wisdom, and it is established by understanding; by knowledge the rooms are filled with every precious and beautiful treasure.

Proverbs 24:3-4 HCSB

— Our Prayer for Today —

Dear Lord, help us to make wise choices, choices that are pleasing to You. Help us to be honest, patient, and kind. And above all, help us to follow the teachings of Jesus, not just today, but every day. Amen

Chapter 70

Look to Christ

Therefore if any man be in Christ, he is a new creature:
old things are passed away;
behold, all things are become new.

2 Corinthians 5:17 KJV

Hannah Whitall Smith spoke to believers of every generation when she advised, "Keep your face upturned to Christ as the flowers do to the sun. Look, and your soul shall live and grow." How true. When we turn our hearts to Jesus, we receive His blessings, His peace, and His grace.

Christ is the ultimate Savior of mankind and the personal Savior of those who believe in Him. As His servants, we should place Him at the very center of our lives, at the center of our marriages, and at the center of our homes. And then, every day that God gives us breath, we should share Christ's love and His message with a world that needs both.

We must think of the Son always, so to speak, streaming forth from the Father, like light from a lamp, or heat from a fire, or thoughts from a mind. He is the self-expression of the Father—what the Father has to say. And there never was a time when He was not saying it.

C. S. Lewis

Look at yourself, or at others, and you will sink; look at Christ, and you can walk on anything.

E. Stanley Jones

If a husband and wife are deeply committed to Jesus Christ, they enjoy enormous advantages over the family with no spiritual dimension.

James Dobson

For the Son of man is come to save that which was lost.

Matthew 18:11 KJV

— Our Prayer for Today —

Dear Jesus, we are humbled by Your love and mercy. You went to Calvary so that we might have eternal life. Thank You, Jesus, for Your priceless gift, and for Your love. You loved us first, Lord, and we will return Your love today and forever. Amen

Chapter 71

A Cause for Celebration

Finally brothers, whatever is true, whatever is honorable,
whatever is just, whatever is pure, whatever is lovely,
whatever is commendable—if there is any moral excellence
and if there is any praise—dwell on these things.

Philippians 4:8 HCSB

A Christian marriage should be cause for celebration, but sometimes we don't feel much like celebrating. In fact, when the weight of the world seems to bear down upon our shoulders, celebration may be the last thing on our minds . . . but it shouldn't be. As God's children, we are all blessed beyond measure on good days and bad. This day is a non-renewable resource—once it's gone, it's gone forever. We should give thanks for this day while using it for the glory of God.

What will your attitude be today? Will you be fearful, angry, bored, or worried? Will you infect your marriage with the twin blights of cynicism and bitterness? Are you a person who celebrates your life and your marriage? Hopefully so! After all, God has richly blessed you, and He wants you to rejoice in His gifts. But, God will not force His joy upon you; you must claim it for yourself.

So today, and every day hereafter, celebrate the life that God has given you. Think optimistically about yourself, your marriage, your family, and your future. Give thanks to the One who has given you everything, and trust in your heart that He wants to give you so much more.

Attitude is all-important. Let the soul take a quiet attitude of faith and love toward God, and from there on, the responsibility is God's. He will make good on His commitments.

A. W. Tozer

Marriage should be many hours of joy interrupted by an occasional minute or two of frustration—not the other way around.

Marie T. Freeman

A miserable heart means a miserable life; a cheerful heart fills the day with a song.

Proverbs 15:15 MSG

— Our Prayer for Today —

We thank You, Lord, for the gift of marriage. And we thank You for the love, the care, the devotion, and the genuine friendship that we share this day and forever. Amen

Chapter 72

Practical Christianity

Therefore, get your minds ready for action,
being self-disciplined, and set your hope completely
on the grace to be brought to you at the revelation
of Jesus Christ.
1 Peter 1:13 HCSB

As Christians, we must do our best to ensure that our actions are accurate reflections of our beliefs. Our theology must be demonstrated, not only by our words but, more importantly, by our actions. In short, we should be practical believers, quick to act whenever we see an opportunity to serve God.

Are you the kind of practical Christian who is willing to dig in and do what needs to be done when it needs to be done? If so, congratulations: God acknowledges your service and blesses it. But if you find yourself more interested in the fine points of theology than in the needs of your neighbors, it's time to rearrange your priorities. God needs believers who are willing to roll up their sleeves and go to work for Him. Count yourself among that number. Theology is a good thing unless it interferes with God's work. And it's up to you to make certain that your theology doesn't.

Do noble things, do not dream them all day long.

Charles Kingsley

A bird does not know it can fly before it uses its wings. We learn God's love in our hearts as soon as we act upon it.

Corrie ten Boom

Action springs not from thought, but from a readiness for responsibility.

Dietrich Bonhoeffer

But be doers of the word and not hearers only.

James 1:22 HCSB

—— Our Prayer for Today ——

Dear Lord, we have heard Your Word, and we have felt Your presence in our hearts; let us act accordingly. Let our words and deeds serve as a testimony to the changes You have made in our lives. Let us praise You, Father, by following in the footsteps of Your Son, and let others see Him through us. Amen

Chapter 73

Total Commitment

*A man leaves his father and mother and bonds
with his wife, and they become one flesh.*

Genesis 2:24 HCSB

Sometimes, it's easy to be in love—just ask any blissful young couple who recently got engaged! But sometimes, love isn't quite as easy as that— just ask any long-married couple who faces health problems, financial difficulties, family tragedy, or any other significant brand of trouble. Honest-to-goodness love is strong enough to weather these storms because honest-to-goodness love isn't a feeling that comes and goes; it's a level of commitment that remains steady and strong, even when times are tough.

Every marriage, like every life, will encounter days of hardship and pain. It is during these difficult days that husbands and wives discover precisely what their marriage is made of.

God's Word makes it clear: genuine love is committed love. Genuine love is more than a feeling . . . it is a decision to make love endure, no matter what. So, if you want your love to last forever, then you and your spouse must be totally committed to each other. When you are, then you can rest assured that the two of you—plus God—can handle anything that comes your way.

Wherever your marriage is today, make or reaffirm your unyielding commitment to its permanence.

Ed Young

Any time you make a commitment to something, it will be tested.

John Maxwell

Marital love is a committed act of the will before it is anything else. It is sacrificial love, a no-turning-back decision.

Ed Young

Wives, be submissive to your husbands, as is fitting in the Lord. Husbands, love your wives and don't become bitter against them.

Colossians 3:18-19 HCSB

— Our Prayer for Today —

Dear Lord, give us the strength and the wisdom to be totally committed to You. Guide us away from the temptations and distractions of this world, so that we might honor You with our thoughts, our actions, and our prayers. Amen

Walk with Him

*Then He said to them all, "If anyone wants to come
with Me, he must deny himself,
take up his cross daily, and follow Me."*

Luke 9:23 HCSB

J esus walks with you. Are you both walking with
Him? Hopefully, you will choose to walk with Him
today and every day of your lives.

Jesus loved you so much that He endured unspeak-
able humiliation and suffering for you. How will you
respond to Christ's sacrifice? Will you take up His cross
and follow Him (Luke 9:23), or will you choose another path? When you place your hopes squarely at the
foot of the cross, when you place Jesus squarely at the
center of your life, you will be blessed. If you seek to be
a worthy disciple of Jesus, you must acknowledge that
He never comes "next." He is always first.

Do you hope to fulfill God's purpose for your lives?
Do you seek lives of abundance and peace? Do you
intend to be Christian not just in name, but in deed?
Then follow Christ. Follow Him by picking up His cross
today and every day that you live. When you do, you
will quickly discover that Christ's love has the power to
change everything, including you.

A disciple is a follower of Christ. That means you take on His priorities as your own. His agenda becomes your agenda. His mission becomes your mission.

Charles Stanley

Think of this—we may live together with Him here and now, a daily walking with Him who loved us and gave Himself for us.

Elisabeth Elliot

When we truly walk with God throughout our day, life slowly starts to fall into place.

Bill Hybels

Then He said to them all, "If anyone wants to come with Me, he must deny himself, take up his cross daily, and follow Me."

Luke 9:23 HCSB

— Our Prayer for Today —

Dear Lord, You sent Your Son so that we might have abundant life and eternal life. Thank You, Father, for our Savior, Christ Jesus. We will follow Him, honor Him, and obey His teachings, this day and every day. Amen

Chapter 75

The Power of Encouragement

Therefore encourage one another and build each other up as you are already doing.

1 Thessalonians 5:11 HCSB

Marriage is a team sport, and all of us need occasional pats on the back from our teammate. In the Book of Proverbs, we read that, "a word aptly spoken is like apples of gold in settings of silver" (25:11 NIV). This verse reminds us that the words we speak can and should be beautiful offerings to those we love.

All of us have the power to enrich the lives of our loved ones. Sometimes, when we feel uplifted and secure, we find it easy to speak words of encouragement and hope. Other times, when we are discouraged or tired, we can scarcely summon the energy to uplift ourselves, much less anyone else. But, as loving Christians, our obligation is clear: we must always measure our words carefully as we use them to benefit others and to glorify our Father in heaven.

God intends that we speak words of kindness, wisdom, and truth, no matter our circumstances, no matter our emotions. When we do, we share a priceless gift with our loved ones, and we give glory to the One who gave His life for us.

Your mate doesn't live by bread alone; he or she needs to be "buttered" from time to time.

Zig Ziglar

Words. Do you fully understand their power? Can any of us really grasp the mighty force behind the things we say? Do we stop and think before we speak, considering the potency of the words we utter?

Joni Eareckson Tada

What are your spouse's dreams? What are you doing to encourage or discourage those dreams?

Dennis Swanberg

Finally, brothers, rejoice. Be restored, be encouraged, be of the same mind, be at peace, and the God of love and peace will be with you.

2 Corinthians 13:11 HCSB

— Our Prayer for Today —

Dear Heavenly Father, because we are Your children, we are blessed. You have loved us eternally, cared for us faithfully, and saved us through the gift of Your Son Jesus. Just as You have lifted us up, Lord, let us lift up others in a spirit of encouragement and optimism and hope. And, if we can help a fellow traveler, even in a small way, Dear Lord, may the glory be Yours. Amen

Chapter 76

Today's Opportunities

Therefore, as we have opportunity,
we must work for the good of all, especially for those
who belong to the household of faith.

Galatians 6:10 HCSB

A re you both excited about the opportunities of today and thrilled by the possibilities of tomorrow? Do you confidently expect God to lead you to a place of abundance, peace, and joy? And, when your days on earth are over, do you expect to receive the priceless gift of eternal life? If you trust God's promises, and if you have welcomed God's Son into your heart, then you believe that your future is intensely and eternally bright.

Today, as you prepare to meet the duties of everyday life, pause and consider God's promises. And then think for a moment about the wonderful future that awaits all believers, including you. God has promised that your future is secure. Trust that promise, and celebrate the life of abundance and eternal joy that is now yours through Christ.

Don't waste today's time cluttering up tomorrow's opportunities with yesterday's troubles.

Barbara Johnson

Life is a glorious opportunity.

Billy Graham

Lovely, complicated wrappings sheath the gift of one-day-more; breathless, I untie the package—never lived this day before!

Gloria Gaither

My cup runs over. Surely goodness and mercy shall follow me all the days of my life; and I will dwell in the house of the Lord forever.

Psalm 23:5-6 NKJV

— Our Prayer for Today —

Dear Lord, as we travel through this life together, we will travel with You. Whatever this day may bring, we will thank You for the opportunity to live abundantly. We will lean upon You, Father—and trust You—this day and forever. Amen

Chapter 77

Time for Silence

Be silent before the Lord and wait expectantly for Him.
Psalm 37:7 HCSB

The world seems to grow louder day by day, and our senses seem to be invaded at every turn. If we allow the distractions of a clamorous society to separate us from God's peace, we do ourselves a profound disservice. Our task, as dutiful believers, is to carve out moments of silence in a world filled with noise.

If we are to maintain righteous minds and compassionate hearts, we must take time each day for prayer and for meditation. We must make ourselves still in the presence of our Creator. We must quiet our minds and our hearts so that we might sense God's will and His love.

Has the busy pace of life robbed you of the peace that God has promised? If so, it's time to reorder your priorities and your life. Nothing is more important than the time you spend with your Heavenly Father. So be still and claim the inner peace that is found in the silent moments you spend with God.

The remedy for distractions is the same now as it was in earlier and simpler times: prayer, meditation, and the cultivation of the inner life.

A. W. Tozer

When an honest soul can get still before the living Christ, we can still hear Him say simply and clearly, "Love the Lord your God with all your heart and with all your soul and with all your mind . . . and love one another as I have loved you."

Gloria Gaither

Be still: pause and discover that God is God.

Charles Swindoll

My soul, wait in silence for God only, for my hope is from Him.

Psalm 62:5 NASB

— Our Prayer for Today —

Dear Lord, in the quiet moments of this day, we will turn our thoughts and prayers to You. In silence we will sense Your presence, and we will seek Your will for our lives, knowing that when we accept Your peace, we will be blessed today and throughout eternity. Amen

Chapter 78

Ultimate Security

*Finally, my brethren, be strong in the Lord
and in the power of His might. Put on the whole armor
of God, that you may be able to stand against
the wiles of the devil.*

Ephesians 6:10-11 NKJV

God is your ultimate source of security. The world offers no safety nets, but God does. He sent His only begotten Son to offer you the priceless gift of eternal life. And now you are challenged to return God's love by obeying His commandments and honoring His Son.

In a world filled with dangers and temptations, God is the ultimate armor. In a world filled with misleading messages, God's Word is the ultimate truth. In a world filled with more frustrations than we can count, God's Son offers the ultimate peace.

Will you and your spouse accept God's peace and wear God's armor against the dangers of our world? Hopefully so—because when you do, you can live courageously, knowing that you possess the ultimate security: God's unfailing love for you.

He goes before us, follows behind us, and hems us safe inside the realm of His protection.

Beth Moore

Our responsibility is to feed from Him, to stay close to Him, to follow Him—because sheep easily go astray—so that we eternally experience the protection and companionship of our Great Shepherd the Lord Jesus Christ.

Franklin Graham

Whether our fear is absolutely realistic or out of proportion in our minds, our greatest refuge is Jesus Christ.

Luci Swindoll

For the eyes of the Lord range throughout the earth to show Himself strong for those whose hearts are completely His.

2 Chronicles 16:9 HCSB

— Our Prayer for Today —

Dear Lord, You have promised never to leave us or forsake us. You are always with us, protecting us and encouraging us. Whatever this day may bring, we thank You for Your love and for Your strength. We will lean upon You, Father, this day and forever. Amen

Chapter 79

The Gift of Life

My purpose is to give life in all its fullness.
John 10:10 HCSB

Life is a glorious gift from God. Treat it that way. This day, like every other, is filled to the brim with opportunities, challenges, and choices. But, no choice that you make is more important than the choice you make concerning God. Today, you will either place Him at the center of your life—or not—and the consequences of that choice have implications that are both temporal and eternal.

Sometimes, we don't intentionally neglect God; we simply allow ourselves to become overwhelmed with the demands of everyday life. And then, without our even realizing it, we gradually drift away from the One we need most. Thankfully, God never drifts away from us. He remains always present, always steadfast, always loving.

As you begin this day, place God and His Son where they belong: in your head, in your prayers, on your lips, and in your heart. And then, with God as your guide and companion, let the journey begin . . .

Life is too short to spend it being angry, bored, or dull.

Barbara Johnson

The moment you come to Christ, the Spirit of God brings the life of God into you, and you begin to live.

Billy Graham

The measure of a life, after all, is not its duration but its donation.

Corrie ten Boom

Seek to lead a quiet life, to mind your own business, and to work with your own hands, as we commanded you.

1 Thessalonians 4:11 HCSB

— Our Prayer for Today —

Dear Lord, You have created this glorious universe, and You have created us. Let us use our lives to Your glory, and let us dedicate our lives to Your Son. Amen

Chapter 80

Celebrating Today

This is the day the LORD has made;
we will rejoice and be glad in it.
Psalm 118:24 NKJV

The 118th Psalm reminds us that today, like every other day, is a cause for celebration. God gives us this day; He fills it to the brim with possibilities, and He challenges us to use it for His purposes. The day is presented to us fresh and clean at midnight, free of charge, but we must beware: Today is a non-renewable resource—once it's gone, it's gone forever. Our responsibility, of course, is to use this day in the service of God's will and according to His commandments.

Today, treasure the time that God has given you. Give Him the glory and the praise and the thanksgiving that He deserves. And search for the hidden possibilities that God has placed along your path. This day is a priceless gift from God, so use it joyfully and encourage others to do likewise. After all, this is the day the Lord has made . . .

If you can forgive the person you were, accept the person you are, and believe in the person you will become, you are headed for joy. So celebrate your life.

Barbara Johnson

Some of us seem so anxious about avoiding hell that we forget to celebrate our journey toward heaven.

Philip Yancey

God has a course mapped out for your life, and all the inadequacies in the world will not change His mind. He will be with you every step of the way. And though it may take time, He has a celebration planned for when you cross over the "Red Seas" of your life.

Charles Swindoll

A cheerful heart has a continual feast.

Proverbs 15:15 HCSB

— Our Prayer for Today —

Dear Lord, help us remember that every day is cause for celebration. Today we will try our best to keep joy in our hearts. We will celebrate the life You have given us here on earth and the eternal life that will be ours in heaven. Amen

Chapter 81

Changes

Listen! I am telling you a mystery: We will not all fall asleep, but we will all be changed, in a moment, in the twinkling of an eye, at the last trumpet. For the trumpet will sound, and the dead will be raised incorruptible, and we will be changed. Because this corruptible must be clothed with incorruptibility, and this mortal must be clothed with immortality. Now when this corruptible is clothed with incorruptibility, and this mortal is clothed with immortality, then the saying that is written will take place: Death has been swallowed up in victory. O Death, where is your victory? O Death, where is your sting?

1 Corinthians 15:51-57 HCSB

The world is in a state of constant change, and so is your family. Kids are growing up and moving out; loved ones are growing older and passing on. Everything around you may seem to be in a state of flux, but you can be comforted: although the world is in a state of constant change, God is not.

If your children seem to be growing up before your eyes, don't panic. And even if other changes in your life are unfolding at a furious pace, your Heavenly Father is the rock that cannot be shaken. His Word promises, "I am the Lord, I do not change" (Malachi 3:6 NKJV).

Remember that "Jesus Christ is the same yesterday, today, and forever" (Hebrews 13:8 NKJV). And rest assured: It is precisely because your Savior does not change that you and your family can face the transitions of life with courage for today and hope for tomorrow.

Conditions are always changing; therefore, I must not be dependent upon conditions. What matters supremely is my soul and my relationship to God.

Corrie ten Boom

The secret of contentment in the midst of change is found in having roots in the changeless Christ—the same yesterday, today and forever.

Ed Young

There is an occasion for everything, and a time for every activity under heaven.

Ecclesiastes 3:1 HCSB

— Our Prayer for Today —

Dear Lord, our family changes, but You are unchanging. When we face the inevitable transitions of life, we will turn to You for strength and assurance. Let our trust in You—like Your love for us—be unchanging and everlasting. Amen

Chapter 82

His Power

*I assure you: The one who believes in Me will also do
the works that I do. And he will do even greater works
than these, because I am going to the Father.
Whatever you ask in My name, I will do it,
so that the Father may be glorified in the Son.
If you ask Me anything in My name, I will do it.*

John 14:12-14 HCSB

When you invite Christ to rule over your heart, you avail yourself of His power. And make no mistake about it: You and Christ, working together, can do miraculous things. In fact, miraculous things are exactly what Christ intends for you to do, but He won't force you to do great things on His behalf. The decision to become a full-fledged participant in His power is a decision that you must make for yourself.

The words of John 14:12 make this promise: when you put absolute faith in Christ, you can share in His power. Today, trust the Savior's promise and expect a miracle in His name.

Look at Christ. He rides not upon a horse which is a steed of war. He comes not with appalling pomp and power but sits upon a donkey, which is a gentle beast to bear burdens and work for men. From this we see that Christ comes not to terrify, to drive, and to oppress, but instead to help and to take for Himself our load.

Martin Luther

The Christian life is not simply following principles but being empowered to fulfill our purpose: knowing and exalting Christ.

Franklin Graham

I pray that the eyes of your heart may be enlightened so you may know what is the hope of His calling, what are the glorious riches of His inheritance among the saints, and what is the immeasurable greatness of His power to us who believe, according to the working of His vast strength.

Ephesians 1:18-19 HCSB

— Our Prayer for Today —

Dear Lord, Your Son died for the salvation of all mankind, and He died for us. Through the power of Christ, we can be compassionate, courageous, and strong. Help us to use that power—inside our marriage and as we reach out together to the world—for the glory of Your kingdom, Father, today and forever. Amen

Chapter 83

Always Humble

Now finally, all of you should be like-minded
and sympathetic, should love believers,
and be compassionate and humble.
1 Peter 3:8 HCSB

God's Word clearly instructs us to be humble. And that's good because, as fallible human beings, we have so very much to be humble about! Yet some of us continue to puff ourselves up, seeming to say, "Look at me!" To do so is wrong.

As Christians, we have been refashioned and saved by Jesus Christ, and that salvation came not because of our own good works but because of God's grace. How, then, can we be prideful? The answer, of course, is that, if we are honest with ourselves and with our God, we simply can't be boastful . . . we must, instead, be eternally grateful and exceedingly humble.

Are you exceedingly humble in every aspect of your life, including your relationships with loved ones? You should be. The good things in your life, including your loved ones, come from God. He deserves the credit—and you deserve the glorious experience of giving it to Him.

Because Christ Jesus came to the world clothed in humility, he will always be found among those who are clothed with humility. He will be found among the humble people.

A. W. Tozer

We are never stronger than the moment we admit we are weak.

Beth Moore

Humility is the fairest and rarest flower that blooms.

Charles Swindoll

Humble yourselves therefore under the mighty hand of God, so that He may exalt you in due time, casting all your care upon Him, because He cares about you.

1 Peter 5:6-7 HCSB

— Our Prayer for Today —

Heavenly Father, Jesus clothed Himself with humility when He chose to leave heaven and come to earth to live and die for us, His children. Jesus is our Master and our example. Clothe us with humility, Lord, so that we might be more like Your Son. Amen

Chapter 84

When Nobody Is Watching

I always do my best to have a clear
conscience toward God and men.
Acts 24:16 HCSB

It has been said that character is what we are when nobody is watching. How true. When we do things that we know aren't right, we try to hide them from our family and friends. But even then, God is watching.

Few things in life torment us more—and few things are more destructive to a marriage—than a guilty conscience. On the other hand, few things in life provide more contentment than the knowledge that we are obeying the conscience that God has placed in our hearts.

If you sincerely want to create the best possible life for yourself and your loved ones, never forsake your conscience. And remember this: when you walk with God, your character will take care of itself . . . and you won't need to look over your shoulder to see who, besides God, is watching.

The beginning of backsliding means your conscience does not answer to the truth.

Oswald Sanders

It is neither safe nor prudent to do anything against one's conscience.

Martin Luther

A good conscience is a continual feast.

Francis Bacon

Let us draw near with a true heart in full assurance of faith, our hearts sprinkled clean from an evil conscience and our bodies washed in pure water.

Hebrews 10:22 HCSB

— Our Prayer for Today —

Dear Lord, You speak to us through the gift of Your Holy Word. And, Father, You speak to us through that still small voice that tells us right from wrong. Let us follow Your way, Lord. And show us Your plans so that we might serve You now and forever. Amen

Chapter 85

The Words We Speak

Therefore, laying aside all malice, all deceit,
hypocrisy, envy, and all evil speaking,
as newborn babes, desire the pure milk of the word,
that you may grow thereby.

1 Peter 2:1-2 NKJV

A ll too often, we underestimate the importance of the words we speak. Whether we realize it or not, our words carry great weight and great power, especially when we are addressing our loved ones.

The Bible reminds us that "reckless words pierce like a sword, but the tongue of the wise brings healing" (Proverbs 12:18 NIV). And Christ taught that "out of the abundance of the heart the mouth speaks" (Matthew 12:34 NKJV).

Does the "abundance of your heart" produce a continuing flow of uplifting words for your loved one? And do you express those feelings many times each day? You should.

When you're angry, do you reign in your tongue? Proverbs 29:11 teaches, "A fool gives full vent to his anger, but a wise man keeps himself under control" (NIV).

So, if you'd like to build a better marriage—and if you'd like to keep building it day by day—think before you speak. Avoid angry outbursts. Refrain from constant criticism. Terminate tantrums. Negate negativism. Cease from being cynical. Instead, use Christ as your guide, and speak words of encouragement, hope, praise, and, above all, love—and speak them often.

The great test of a man's character is his tongue.

Oswald Chambers

Change the heart, and you change the speech.

Warren Wiersbe

No rotten talk should come from your mouth, but only what is good for the building up of someone in need, in order to give grace to those who hear.

Ephesians 4:29 HCSB

— Our Prayer for Today —

Dear Lord, You have warned us that we will be judged by the words we speak. Keep us mindful that we have influence on many people, and let the words that we speak today be worthy of the One who has saved us forever. Amen

Chapter 86

Courtesy Matters

Dear friend, you are showing your faith by whatever you do for the brothers, and this you are doing for strangers.

3 John 1:5 HCSB

Did Christ instruct us in matters of etiquette and courtesy? Of course He did. Christ's instructions are clear: "In everything, therefore, treat people the same way you want them to treat you, for this is the Law and the Prophets" (Matthew 7:12 NASB). Jesus did not say, "In some things, treat people as you wish to be treated." And, He did not say, "From time to time, treat others with kindness." Christ said that we should treat others as we wish to be treated in every aspect of our daily lives. This, of course, is a tall order indeed, but as Christians, we are commanded to do our best.

Today, be a little kinder than necessary to your spouse, to family members, to friends, and to total strangers. And, as you consider all the things that Christ has done in your life, honor Him with your words and with your deeds. He expects no less, and He deserves no less.

Only the courteous can love, but it is love that makes them courteous.

C. S. Lewis

Courtesy is contagious.

Marie T. Freeman

When you extend hospitality to others, you're not trying to impress people; you're trying to reflect God to them.

Max Lucado

Don't neglect to show hospitality, for by doing this some have welcomed angels as guests without knowing it.

Hebrews 13:2 HCSB

— Our Prayer for Today —

Help us, Lord, to treat everyone—especially each other—with courtesy and respect. You have created each person in Your own image; we are all Your children, Father. So let us show kindness to all. Amen

Chapter 87

Learning His Lessons

An ear that listens to life-giving rebukes
will be at home among the wise.
Proverbs 15:31 HCSB

One way that we learn about God is by learning
the lessons that He is trying so desperately
to teach us. But when it comes to learning
God's lessons, most of us can be quite hardheaded.
Why? Because we are, by nature, stubborn creatures;
and because we seem destined, at times, to make things
hard on ourselves.

As we go about the business of learning life's lessons,
we can either do things the easy way or the hard way.
The easy way can be summed up as follows: when God
tries to teach us something, we learn it . . . the first
time! Unfortunately, too many of us learn much more
slowly than that.

When we resist God's instruction, He continues to
teach, whether we like it or not. Our challenge, then,
is to discern God's lessons from the experiences of
everyday life. Hopefully, we learn those lessons sooner
rather than later because the sooner we do so, the
sooner He can move on to the next lesson and the next
and the next . . .

The wonderful thing about God's schoolroom is that we get to grade our own papers. You see, He doesn't test us so He can learn how well we're doing. He tests us so we can discover how well we're doing.

Charles Swindoll

The wise man gives proper appreciation in his life to his past. He learns to sift the sawdust of heritage in order to find the nuggets that make the current moment have any meaning.

Grady Nutt

I hope you don't mind me telling you all this? One can learn only by seeing one's mistakes.

C. S. Lewis

Even zeal is not good without knowledge, and the one who acts hastily sins.

Proverbs 19:2 HCSB

— Our Prayer for Today —

Dear Lord, we have so much to learn. Help us to watch, to listen, to think, and to learn every day of our lives. Amen

Chapter 88

Beyond the Disappointments

For you need endurance, so that after you have done God's will, you may receive what was promised.

Hebrews 10:36 HCSB

The occasional disappointments and failures of life are inevitable. Such setbacks are simply the price that we must occasionally pay for our willingness to take risks as we follow our dreams. But even when we encounter bitter disappointments, we must never lose faith.

The reassuring words of Hebrews 10:36 remind us that when we persevere, we will eventually receive that which God has promised. What's required is perseverance, not perfection.

When we encounter the inevitable difficulties of life here on earth, God stands ready to protect us. Our responsibility, of course, is to ask Him for protection. When we call upon Him in heartfelt prayer, He will answer—in His own time and according to His own plan—and He will heal us. And, while we are waiting for God's plans to unfold and for His healing touch to restore us, we can be comforted in the knowledge that our Creator can overcome any obstacle, even if we cannot.

One of the ways God refills us after failure is through the blessing of Christian fellowship. Just experiencing the joy of simple activities shared with other children of God can have a healing effect on us.

Anne Graham Lotz

The almighty Father will use life's reverses to move you forward.

Barbara Johnson

Never imagine that you can be a loser by trusting in God.

C. H. Spurgeon

Blessed is a man who endures trials, because when he passes the test he will receive the crown of life that He has promised to those who love Him.

James 1:12 HCSB

— Our Prayer for Today —

Dear Lord, when we encounter failures and disappointments, keep us mindful that You are in control. Let us persevere— even if our souls are troubled—and let us follow Your Son, Jesus Christ, this day and forever. Amen

Chapter 89

The Right Kind of Fear

Honor all people. Love the brotherhood.
Fear God. Honor the king.
1 Peter 2:17 NKJV

Do you both have a healthy, fearful respect for God's power? If so, you are wise because real wisdom begins with a profound appreciation for God's limitless power.

God praises humility and punishes pride. That's why God's greatest servants will always be those humble men and women who care less for their own glory and more for God's glory. In God's kingdom, the only way to achieve greatness is to shun it. And the only way to be wise is to understand these facts: God is great; He is all-knowing; and He is all-powerful. We must respect Him, and we must humbly obey His commandments, or we must accept the consequences of our misplaced pride.

When true believers are awed by the greatness of God and by the privilege of becoming His children, then they become sincerely motivated, effective evangelists.

Bill Hybels

A healthy fear of God will do much to deter us from sin.

Charles Swindoll

The fear of God is the death of every other fear.

C. H. Spurgeon

When all has been heard, the conclusion of the matter is: fear God and keep His commands.

Ecclesiastes 12:13 HCSB

— Our Prayer for Today —

Lord, You love us and protect us. We praise You, Father, for Your grace, and we respect You for Your infinite power. Let our greatest fear in life be the fear of displeasing You. Amen

Chapter 90

The Art of Cooperation

And if a kingdom be divided against itself,
that kingdom cannot stand. And if a house be divided
against itself, that house cannot stand.

Mark 3:24-25 KJV

Have you and your mate learned the art of cooperation? If so, you have learned the wisdom of "give and take," not the foolishness of "me first." Cooperation is the art of compromising on many little things while keeping your eye on one big thing: your relationship.

Cooperative relationships flourish over time. But, whenever couples fail to cooperate with each other, they sow the seeds of dissatisfaction, frustration, and competition within their marriage. In such cases, marriage partners may find themselves engaged in an unwitting "contest" to receive their "fair share" from the relationship. These types of struggles inevitably create far more problems than they solve.

If you're like most of us, you're probably a little bit headstrong: you probably want most things done in a fashion resembling the popular song "My Way." But, if you are observant, you will notice that those people who always insist upon "my way or the highway" usually end up with "the highway."

A better strategy for all concerned (including you) is to abandon the search for "my way" and search instead for "our way." The best marriages are those in which both partners learn how to "give and take" . . . with both partners trying to give a little more than they take.

Being committed to one's mate is not a matter of demanding rights, but a matter of releasing rights.

Charles Swindoll

Coming together is a beginning. Keeping together is progress. Working together is success.

John Maxwell

Blessed are the peacemakers, because they will be called sons of God.

Matthew 5:9 HCSB

— Our Prayer for Today —

Lord, so much more can be accomplished when we join together to fulfill our common goals. As we seek to fulfill Your will for our lives, let us also join with others to accomplish Your greater good for our families, for our communities, for our nation, and for our world. Amen

Chapter 91

Financial Common Sense

How much better to get wisdom than gold!
And to get understanding is to be chosen rather than silver.
Proverbs 16:16 NKJV

Face facts: it's important for couples to manage money wisely. And it's important to pass on money-management skills to your kids.

Countless books have been written about money—how to make it and how to keep it. But you probably already own at least one copy—and probably several copies—of the world's foremost guide to financial security. That book is the Holy Bible. God's Word is not only a roadmap to eternal life, but it is also an indispensable guidebook for life here on earth. As such, the Bible has much to say about your faith and your finances.

God's Word promises that when you sow generously, you will reap generously (2 Corinthians 9:6). And the Bible promises that when you behave wisely, you'll be rewarded (Proverbs 16:20). So if you'd like to improve your family's finances, or any other aspect of your life, read God's instruction book and follow it to the letter. When you do, you'll be blessed today, tomorrow, and every day of your life.

Virtually everything we see in the area of finances is little more than an external reflection of the internal spiritual condition.

Larry Burkett

If your outgo exceeds your income, then your upkeep will be your downfall.

John Maxwell

Sadly, family problems and even financial problems are seldom the real problem, but often the symptom of a weak or nonexistent value system.

Dave Ramsey

And my God shall supply all your need according to His riches in glory by Christ Jesus.

Philippians 4:19 NKJV

— Our Prayer for Today —

Lord, there are many things we desire, and many things we may never have. But we can have peace. We will trust You to care for our needs, Father, today, tomorrow, and forever. Amen

Chapter 92

Fitness Matters

Therefore, whether you eat or drink, or whatever you do, do everything for God's glory.

1 Corinthians 10:31 HCSB

Physical fitness requires discipline: the discipline to exercise regularly and the discipline to eat sensibly—it's as simple as that. But here's the catch: understanding the need for discipline is easy, but leading a disciplined life can be hard for most of us. Why? Because it's usually more fun to eat a second piece of cake than it is to jog a second lap around the track. But, as we survey the second helpings that all too often find their way on to our plates, we should consider this: when we behave in undisciplined ways, we inevitably suffer.

Are you both choosing to treat your bodies like temples? Hopefully so because physical fitness is a choice—a choice that determines how well you live and how long you live. So treat your bodies like one-of-a-kind gifts from God . . . because that's precisely what they are.

Whenever I read the words of Isaiah that say those who "wait on the Lord" shall "run and not be weary" and "walk and not faint," I'm reminded of how naturally spiritual development and endurance exercise go together.

Dr. Kenneth Cooper

You can look at your calorie count in the same way you might look at a bank account. Every mouthful of food is a deposit and every activity that requires energy is a withdrawal. If we deposit more than we withdraw our surplus grows larger and larger.

Jim Maxwell

Do you not know that your body is a sanctuary of the Holy Spirit who is in you, whom you have from God? You are not your own, for you were bought at a price; therefore glorify God in your body.

1 Corinthians 6:19-20 HCSB

— Our Prayer for Today —

Lord, all that we are belongs to You. As we serve You with all that we are and all that we have, help us honor You by caring for the bodies that You have given us. Amen

Chapter 93

Ask Him

Be anxious for nothing, but in everything by prayer
and supplication, with thanksgiving,
let your requests be made known to God.
Philippians 4:6 NKJV

How often do you ask for God's help? Occasionally? Intermittently? Whenever you experience a crisis? Hopefully not. Hopefully, you and your spouse have developed the habit of asking for God's assistance early and often. And hopefully, you have learned to seek His guidance in every aspect of your life.

God has promised that when you ask for His help, He will not withhold it. So ask. Ask Him to meet the needs of your day. Ask Him for wisdom. Ask Him to lead you, to protect you, and to correct you. And trust the answers He gives.

God stands at the door and waits. When you knock on His door, He answers. Your task, of course, is to seek His guidance prayerfully, confidently, and often.

Notice that we must ask. And we will sometimes struggle to hear and struggle with what we hear. But personally, it's worth it. I'm after the path of life—and he alone knows it.

John Eldredge

Some people think God does not like to be troubled with our constant asking. But, the way to trouble God is not to come at all.

D. L. Moody

When will we realize that we're not troubling God with our questions and concerns? His heart is open to hear us—his touch nearer than our next thought—as if no one in the world existed but us. Our very personal God wants to hear from us personally.

Gigi Graham Tchividjian

Now if any of you lacks wisdom, he should ask God, who gives to all generously and without criticizing, and it will be given to him.

James 1:5 HCSB

— Our Prayer for Today —

Dear Lord, You are the giver of all things good. When we are in need, we will come to You in prayer. You know the desires of our hearts, Lord; grant them, we ask. Yet not our will, Father, but Your will be done. Amen

Chapter 94

The Importance of Fellowship

Now I urge you, brothers, in the name of our Lord Jesus Christ, that you all say the same thing, that there be no divisions among you, and that you be united with the same understanding and the same conviction.

1 Corinthians 1:10 HCSB

Fellowship with other believers should be an integral part of your lives and your marriage. Your association with fellow Christians should be uplifting, enlightening, encouraging, and consistent.

Are you both active members of your fellowship? Are you builders of bridges inside the four walls of your church and outside it? Do you contribute to God's glory by contributing your time and your talents to a close-knit band of believers? Hopefully so. The fellowship of believers is intended to be a powerful tool for spreading God's Good News and uplifting His children. And God intends for you both to be fully contributing members of that fellowship. Your intentions should be the same.

God shows unbridled delight when He sees people acting in ways that honor Him: when He receives worship, when He sees faith demonstrated in the most trying of circumstances, and when He sees tender love shared among His people.

Bill Hybels

In God's economy you will be hard-pressed to find many examples of successful "Lone Rangers."

Luci Swindoll

The Lord Jesus Christ enables us all to be family.

Dennis Swanberg

Do not be unequally yoked together with unbelievers. For what fellowship has righteousness with lawlessness? And what communion has light with darkness?

2 Corinthians 6:14 NKJV

— Our Prayer for Today —

Heavenly Father, You have given us a community of supporters called the church. Let our fellowship be a reflection of the love we feel for each other, the love we feel for our fellow believers, and the love we feel for You. Amen

Chapter 95

Priorities

*But whoever listens to me will live securely
and be free from the fear of danger.*

Proverbs 1:33 HCSB

It takes time to build a strong marriage . . . lots of time. Yet we live in a world where time seems to be an ever-shrinking commodity as we rush from place to place with seldom a moment to spare.

Has the busy pace of life robbed you of sufficient time with your loved ones? If so, it's time to adjust your priorities. And God can help.

When you fervently ask God to you help prioritize your life, He will give you guidance. When you seek His guidance every day, your Creator will reveal Himself in a variety of ways. As a follower of Christ, you must do no less.

When you allow God to help you organize your day, you'll soon discover that there is ample time for your spouse and your family. When you make God a full partner in every aspect of your life, He will lead you along the proper path: His path. When you allow God to reign over your heart, He will honor you with spiritual blessings that are simply too numerous to count. So, as you plan for the day ahead, make God's priorities your priorities. When you do, every other priority will have a tendency to fall neatly into place.

Oh, that we might discern the will of God, surrender to His calling, resign the masses of activities, and do a few things well. What a legacy that would be for our children.

Beth Moore

The moment you wake up each morning, all your wishes and hopes for the day rush at you like wild animals. And the first job each morning consists in shoving it all back; in listening to that other voice, taking that other point of view, letting that other, larger, stronger, quieter life coming flowing in.

C. S. Lewis

Give me the person who says, "This one thing I do, and not these fifty things I dabble in."

D. L. Moody

And I pray this: that your love will keep on growing in knowledge and every kind of discernment, so that you can determine what really matters and can be pure and blameless in the day of Christ.

Philippians 1:9 HCSB

— Our Prayer for Today —

Dear Lord, let Your priorities be our priorities. Let Your will be our will. Let Your Word be our guide, and let us grow in faith and in wisdom this day and every day. Amen

Chapter 96

Generosity Now

Based on the gift they have received,
everyone should use it to serve others,
as good managers of the varied grace of God.
1 Peter 4:10 HCSB

Hymn writer Fanny Crosby wrote, "To God be the glory; great thing He hath done! So loved He the world that He gave us his son." God's love for us is so complete that He sent Jesus to this earth so that we, His believers, might have eternal life: "But God demonstrates his own love for us in this: While we were still sinners, Christ died for us" (Romans 5:8 NIV).

We, as Christ's followers, are challenged to share His love. We do so, in part, by dealing generously and lovingly with others.

When we walk each day with Christ—and obey the commandments found in God's Holy Word—we are worthy ambassadors for Him. Just as Christ has been—and will always be—the ultimate Friend to His flock, so should we be Christlike in our love and generosity to those in pain and to those in need. When we share the love of Christ, we share a priceless gift; may we share it today and every day that we live.

The happiest and most joyful people are those who give money and serve.

Dave Ramsey

Here lies the tremendous mystery—that God should be all-powerful, yet refuse to coerce. He summons us to cooperation. We are honored in being given the opportunity to participate in His good deeds. Remember how He asked for help in performing His miracles: Fill the water pots, stretch out your hand, distribute the loaves.

Elisabeth Elliot

Remember this: the person who sows sparingly will also reap sparingly, and the person who sows generously will also reap generously. Each person should do as he has decided in his heart—not out of regret or out of necessity, for God loves a cheerful giver. And God is able to make every grace overflow to you, so that in every way, always having everything you need, you may excel in every good work.

2 Corinthians 9:6-8 HCSB

— Our Prayer for Today —

Dear Lord, You have been so generous with us; let us be generous with others. Help us to focus on the needs of others. And, make us humble givers, Lord, so that all the glory and the praise might be Yours. Amen

Quick to Judge?

Do not judge, and you will not be judged.
Do not condemn, and you will not be condemned.
Forgive, and you will be forgiven.

Luke 6:37 HCSB

We have all fallen short of God's commandments, and He has forgiven us. We, too, must forgive others. And, we must refrain from judging them.

Are you one of those people who finds it easy to judge others? If so, it's time to change.

God does not need (or, for that matter, want) your help. Why? Because God is perfectly capable of judging the human heart . . . while you are not.

As Christians, we are warned that to judge others is to invite fearful consequences: to the extent we judge others, so, too, will we be judged by God. Let us refrain, then, from judging our neighbors. Instead, let us forgive them and love them in the same way that God has forgiven us.

Being critical of others, including God, is one way we try to avoid facing and judging our own sins.

Warren Wiersbe

Don't judge other people more harshly than you want God to judge you.

Marie T. Freeman

Judging draws the judgment of others.

Catherine Marshall

Why do you look at the speck in your brother's eye, but don't notice the log in your own eye? Or how can you say to your brother, "Let me take the speck out of your eye," and look, there's a log in your eye? Hypocrite! First take the log out of your eye, and then you will see clearly to take the speck out of your brother's eye.

Matthew 7:3-5 HCSB

— Our Prayer for Today —

Dear Lord, sometimes we are quick to judge others. But, You have commanded us not to judge. Keep us mindful, Father, that when we judge others, we are living outside Your will for our lives. You have forgiven us, Lord. Let us forgive others, let us love them, and let us help them . . . without judging them. Amen

Chapter 98

Saved by Grace

But God, who is abundant in mercy,
because of His great love that He had for us,
made us alive with the Messiah even though we were
dead in trespasses. By grace you are saved!

Ephesians 2:4-5 HCSB

We are saved, not by our own righteousness, but by God's grace. God's priceless gift of eternal life is not a reward for our good deeds; it is a manifestation of God's infinite love for those who worship Him and accept His Son as their Savior.

Are you absolutely certain that you have accepted the gift of salvation? If not, drop to your knees this very instant and accept Christ as your personal Savior. And, if you are already the thankful recipient of eternal life through Christ Jesus, use this day as an opportunity to share your testimony with friends and family members.

Jesus is the sovereign Friend and ultimate Savior of mankind. Christ showed enduring love for us by willingly sacrificing His own life so that we might have eternal life. Let us love Him, praise Him, and share His message of salvation with our neighbors and with the world.

The grace of God is infinite and eternal. As it had no beginning, so it can have no end, and being an attribute of God, it is as boundless as infinitude.

A. W. Tozer

Jesus has affected human society like no other. The incomparable Christ is the good news. And what makes it such good news is that man is so undeserving but that God is so gracious.

John MacArthur

The grace of God is sufficient for all our needs, for every problem, and for every difficulty, for every broken heart, and for every human sorrow.

Peter Marshall

My grace is sufficient for you, for My strength is made perfect in weakness.

2 Corinthians 12:9 NKJV

— Our Prayer for Today —

Lord, Your grace is a gift that cannot be earned. It is a gift that was given freely when we accepted Your Son as our personal Savior. Freely have we received Your gifts, Father. Let us freely share our gifts, our possessions, our time, our energy, and our faith. And let us bring honor to You and to Your Son, now and forever. Amen

Chapter 99

The Ultimate Protection

*I know whom I have believed and am persuaded
that He is able to guard what has been entrusted
to me until that day.*

2 Timothy 1:12 HCSB

The hand of God encircles us and comforts us in times of adversity. In times of hardship, He restores our strength; in times of sorrow, He dries our tears. When we are troubled or weak or embittered, God is as near as our next breath.

God has promised to protect us, and He intends to fulfill His promise. In a world filled with dangers and temptations, God is the ultimate armor. In a world filled with misleading messages, God's Word is the ultimate truth. In a world filled with more frustrations than we can count, God's Son offers the ultimate peace.

Will you accept God's peace and wear God's armor against the dangers of our world? Hopefully so, because when you do, you can live courageously, knowing that you possess the ultimate protection: God's unfailing love for you.

The Rock of Ages is the great sheltering encirclement.

Oswald Chambers

Prayer is our pathway not only to divine protection, but also to a personal, intimate relationship with God.

Shirley Dobson

There is no safer place to live than the center of His will.

Calvin Miller

The Lord is my rock, my fortress, and my deliverer.

Psalm 18:2 HCSB

— Our Prayer for Today —

Lord, You are our Shepherd. You care for us; You comfort us; You watch over us; and You have saved us. We will praise You, Father, for Your glorious works, for Your protection, for Your love, and for Your Son. Amen

Chapter 100

Personally Acquainted

And Jesus said to them, "I am the bread of life.
He who comes to Me shall never hunger,
and he who believes in Me shall never thirst."

John 6:35 NKJV

The 19th-century writer Hannah Whitall Smith observed, "The crucial question for each of us is this: What do you think of Jesus, and do you yet have a personal acquaintance with Him?" Indeed, the answer to that question determines the quality, the course, and the direction of our lives today and for all eternity.

The old familiar hymn begins, "What a friend we have in Jesus . . . " No truer words were ever penned. Christ showed enduring love for His believers by willingly sacrificing His own life so that we might have life eternal. Now, it is our turn to become His friend.

Let us love our Savior, praise Him, and share His message of salvation with our neighbors and with the world. When we do, we demonstrate that our acquaintance with the Master is not a passing fancy; it is, instead, the cornerstone of our marriages and the touchstone of our lives.

Jesus makes God visible. But that truth does not make Him somehow less than God. He is equally supreme with God.

Anne Graham Lotz

In your greatest weakness, turn to your greatest strength, Jesus, and hear Him say, "My grace is sufficient for you, for My strength is made perfect in weakness" (2 Corinthians 12:9 NKJV).

Lisa Whelchel

At the name of Jesus every knee should bow, of those in heaven, and of those on earth, and of those under the earth, and that every tongue should confess that Jesus Christ is Lord, to the glory of God the Father.

Philippians 2:10-11 NKJV

— Our Prayer for Today —

Thank You, Lord, for Your Son Jesus. You loved this world so dearly, Father, that You sent Your Son to die so that we, Your children, might have life eternal. We praise You for that priceless gift. Let the love of Jesus be reflected in our words, our thoughts, and our deeds. And, let us share His transforming message with a world in desperate need of His peace. Amen

Now these three remain:
faith, hope, and love.
But the greatest of these is love.

—

1 Corinthians 13:13 HCSB